INDEX TO
THE PROCEEDINGS OF THE
BRITISH ACADEMY

Volumes 1–63

INDEX TO THE
PROCEEDINGS OF THE
BRITISH ACADEMY, London

Volumes 1–63

COMPILED BY

MICHAEL HOPE

LONDON
PUBLISHED FOR THE BRITISH ACADEMY
BY THE OXFORD UNIVERSITY PRESS
1980

Oxford University Press, Walton Street, Oxford OX2 6DP

OXFORD LONDON GLASGOW
NEW YORK TORONTO MELBOURNE WELLINGTON
KUALA LUMPUR SINGAPORE HONG KONG TOKYO
DELHI BOMBAY CALCUTTA MADRAS KARACHI
NAIROBI DAR ES SALAAM CAPE TOWN

Published in the United States by
Oxford University Press, New York

ISBN 0 19 725999 5

A reprint edition of volumes 1–50 is available from Kraus Reprint, FL-9491 Nendeln, Liechtenstein. Other volumes are available from the British Academy. Offprints of many lectures and memoirs may also be obtained from the Academy.

Printed in Great Britain
at the University Press, Oxford
by Eric Buckley
Printer to the University

CONTENTS

PREFACE

This Index covers the first sixty-three volumes of the *Proceedings of the British Academy*. It has been prepared in three sections: an index of authors, an index of memoirs, and an index of titles and principal subjects. No attempt has been made in the last to index the contents of each paper in detail, but all titles have been given; where the first word of the title does not appear to give sufficient clue to its contents a second entry has been provided under the heading of the principal subject. Proper names, whether of authors or subjects, have been entered under the initial letter of the surname, ignoring Christian names and titles. The words 'The' 'A' and 'On' have been ignored in entering the initial word of a title. A bold arabic figure following an entry refers to the number of the volume in which the lecture or memoir may be found, and the next figure to the page in that volume. The Index follows the pagination of the original Academy volumes throughout. The Kraus reprint of volumes 1–50 has identical pagination, except in the case of volume 2.

MICHAEL HOPE

LIST OF ABBREVIATIONS

AA	Lecture on Aspects of Art (Henriette Hertz Trust)
AR	Albert Reckitt Archaeological Lecture
C	Chatterton Lecture on an English Poet
DH	Dawes Hicks Lecture on Philosophy
E	Biennial Lecture on English Literature (Mrs Frida Monti Trust)
Ex. A	Exchange lecture with the University of Athens
IG	Sir Israel Gollancz Memorial Lecture
JR	Sir John Rhys Memorial Lecture
K	Keynes Lecture in Economics
Mac	Maccabaean Lecture in Jurisprudence
MM	Lecture on a Master-Mind (Henriette Hertz Trust)
MW	Mortimer Wheeler Archaeological Lecture
P	Philosophical Lecture (Henriette Hertz Trust)
R	Raleigh Lecture on History (Viscount Wakefield Foundation)
RB	Radcliffe-Brown Lecture in Social Anthropology
S	Shakespeare Lecture (English Literature & Language Foundation)
STP	Sarah Tryphena Phillips Lecture in American Literature and History
TOB	Thank-offering to Britain Fund Lecture
W	Warton Lecture on English Poetry (English Literature & Language Foundation)

INDEX OF AUTHORS

A

AARON, R. I.
Our Knowledge of Universals (P)
31, 17

ABBOTT, Revd. Edwin A.
'Righteousness' in the Gospels
8, 351

ABERCROMBIE, Lascelles
A Plea for the Liberty of Interpreting (S)
16, 137

ABRAHAM, Gerald
(Sir) Jack Allan Westrup, 1904–75. Obituary
63, 471

ACKRILL, J. L.
Aristotle on *Eudaimonia* (DH)
60, 439

ACTON, H. B.
The Philosophy of Language in Revolutionary France (DH)
45, 199

ADCOCK, Sir Frank E.
James Smith Reid, 1846–1926. Obituary.
13, 335
(Revd.) Martin Percival Charlesworth, 1895–1950. Obituary
36, 277
Greek and Macedonian Kingship (R)
39, 163
Sir William Woodthorpe Tarn, 1869–1957. Obituary
44, 253
William Henry Samuel Jones, 1876–1963. Obituary
49, 413

ADY, C. M.
Morals and Manners of the Quattrocento (I)
28, 179

ALBA, The Duke of
The Pharos of Alexandria—Summary of an Essay in Spanish by Don Miguel de Asin
19, 277

ALEXANDER, Nigel
The Performance of Christopher Marlowe's *Dr. Faustus* (C)
57, 331

ALEXANDER, Peter
Shakespeare's Punctuation (S)
31, 61

ALEXANDER, Samuel
The Basis of Realism
6, 279
Artistic Creation and Cosmic Creation (P)
13, 247

ALLAN, D. J.
Guy Cromwell Field, 1887–1955. Obituary
42, 311

ALLBUTT, Sir Thomas Clifford
Palissy, Bacon and the Revival of Natural Science
6, 233

ALLEN, P. S.
Erasmus' Services to Learning (MM)
11, 349
Charles Plummer, 1851–1927. Obituary
15, 463

ALLEN, T. W.
Greek Abbreviation in the Fifteenth Century
12, 55
The Homeric Scholia
17, 179
Arthur Ernest Cowley, 1861–1931. Obituary
19, 351
Theognis
20, 71

ALLEN, W. E.
Some Aspects of the American Short Story (STP)
59, 125

ALVORD, Clarence Walworth
Lord Shelburne and the Founding of British-American Goodwill (R)
11, 369

ANDERSON, Revd. G. W.
(Revd.) Harold Henry Rowley, 1890–1969. Obituary
56, 309

ANDREWES, Antony
Theodore Wade-Gery, 1888–1972. Obituary
59, 419

ANSCOMBE, G. E. M. (Mrs P. T. Geach)
Times, Beginnings, and Causes (P)
60, 253

ARCHBOLD, W. A. J.
Lord Acton as a Cambridge Professor. Obituary   **1**, 282
ARMSTRONG, Edward
Edward Moore, 1835–1916. Obituary   **7**, 575
History and Art in the Quattrocento (I)   **10**, 415
ARMSTRONG, Sir William
The Role and Character of the Civil Service (TOB)   **56**, 209
ASHBY, Sir Eric
The Academic Profession (TOB)   **55**, 163
ASHMOLE, Bernard
Late Archaic and Early Classical Greek Sculpture in Sicily and South Italy (AA)   **20**, 91
Cyriac of Ancona (I)   **45**, 25
Some Nameless Sculptures of the Fifth Century BC (AA)   **48**, 213
Sir John Beazley, 1885–1970. Obituary   **56**, 443
ASHTON, T. S.
Changes in Standards of Comfort in Eighteenth-century England (R)   **41**, 171
Richard Henry Tawney, 1880–1962. Obituary   **48**, 461
ASIN, Don Miguel de
The Pharos of Alexandria   **19**, 277
ASPINALL, A.
The Cabinet Council 1783–1835 (R)   **38**, 145
AUSTIN, J. L.
Ifs and Cans (P)   **42**, 109
AYER, Sir Alfred J.
Privacy (P)   **45**, 43
Bertrand Russell as a Philosopher (MM)   **58**, 127

B

BAILEY, Cyril
Robert Seymour Conway, 1864–1933. Obituary   **22**, 434
Albert Curtis Clark, 1859–1937. Obituary   **23**, 513

John William Mackail, OM 1859–1945. Obituary   **31**, 245
Lucretius (MM)   **35**, 143
Sir Arthur Wallace Pickard-Cambridge, 1873–1952. Obituary   **38**, 303
BAILEY, John
Poetry and Commonplace (W)   **9**, 213
BAILEY, S. J.
(Sir) Percy Henry Winfield, 1878–1953. Obituary   **41**, 329
BAILLIE, J. B.
Andrew Seth Pringle-Pattison, 1856–1931. Obituary   **17**, 447
BALFOUR, The Earl of
Familiar Beliefs and Transcendent Reason (P)   **11**, 395
BALL, C. J.
Shumer and Shem: some Philological Coincidences and Sequences   **7**, 85
BARKER, E.
Leonard Trelawney Hobhouse, 1864–1929. Obituary   **15**, 536
BARNETT, L. D.
Edward James Rapson, 1861–1937. Obituary   **23**, 526
BARNS, J. W. B.
A new Psalms Fragment   **43**, 229
BARRÈS, Maurice
Le Blason de la France, ou ses traits éternels dans cette guerre et dans les vieilles épopées (AC)   **7**, 339
BARRETT, Revd. C. K.
(Revd.) Vincent Taylor, 1887–1968. Obituary   **56**, 283
BARRETT, Douglas
The Dancing Siva in Early South Indian Art (MW)   **62**, 181
BASHAM, A. L.
Lionel David Barnett, 1871–1960. Obituary   **46**, 333
BATE, H. N.
Frank Edward Brightman, 1856–1932. Obituary   **19**, 345
BATHO, Edith C.
The Poet and the Past (W)   **23**, 29

BAYLEY, John
Keats and Reality (C) **48**, 91
BAYNES, Norman H.
John Bagnell Bury, 1861–1927.
Obituary **13**, 368
Constantine the Great and the
Christian Church (R) **15**, 341
BEASLEY, W. G.
Japan and the West in the Mid-
Nineteenth Century (R) **55**, 77
BEAZLEY, Sir John D.
Attic Black-Figure (AA) **14**, 217
Potter and Painter in Ancient
Athens **30**, 87
Some Attic Vases in the Cyprus
Museum **33**, 195
'ΕΛΕΝΗΣ 'ΑΠΑΙΤΗΣΙΣ **43**, 233
BEECHING, The Very Revd. H. C.,
Dean of Norwich
The Character of Shakespeare (S)
8, 157
BEER, John
Milton, Lost and Regained (C)
50, 143
BELL, Sir Harold Idris
Magical Texts from a Bilingual
Papyrus in the British Museum
17, 235
Arthur Surridge Hunt, 1871–1934.
Obituary **20**, 323
Robin Ernest William Flower,
1881–1946. Obituary **32**, 353
Presidential Address, 16 July 1947
33, 19
Presidential Address, 14 July 1948
34, 15
Walter Ewing Crum, 1865–1944.
Obituary **34**, 281
Presidential Address, 13 July 1949
35, 15
Presidential Address, 12 July 1950
36, 15
Sir Frederick George Kenyon, 1863–
1952. Obituary **38**, 269
The Welsh Literary Renascence of
the Twentieth Century (JR)
39, 139
BENNETT, H. S.
Shakespeare's Audience (S) **30**, 73

George Gordon Coulton, 1858–
1947. Obituary **33**, 267
BENNETT, Joan
Poetry and Interpretation (W)
44, 185
BERGIN, Osborn
The Native Irish Grammarian (JR)
24, 205
BERKELEY, G. F-H.
Some fresh documents concerning
the Italian Risorgimento before
1849 (I) **26**, 227
BERLIN, Sir Isaiah
Montesquieu **41**, 267
Presidential Address, 10 July 1975
61, 71
Presidential Address, 1 July 1976
62, 85
Presidential Address, 30 June 1977
63, 1
BERNARD, The Very Revd. J. H.
Dr George Salmon. Obituary
1, 311
BERNARD, Paul
Aï Khanum on the Oxus.: a Hellen-
istic City in Central Asia (AR)
53, 71
BETHUNE-BAKER, Revd. J. F.
Francis Crawford Burkitt, 1864–
1935. Obituary **22**, 445
(Revd.) Alan England Brooke,
1863–1939. Obituary **26**, 439
(Revd.) John Martin Creed, 1889–
1940. Obituary **26**, 517
BEZZANT, Revd. Canon J. S.
The Very Reverend Norman Sykes,
1897–1961. Obituary **47**, 417
BICKERSTETH, Geoffrey L.
Leopardi and Wordsworth (I)
13, 47
The Golden World of 'King Lear'
(S) **32**, 147
BINCHY, D. A.
The Linguistic and Historical Value
of the Irish Law Tracts (JR)
29, 195
BINDOFF, S. T.
(Sir) Charles Kingsley Webster,
1886–1961. Obituary **48**, 427

BINYON, Laurence
English Poetry in its Relation to Painting and the other Arts (AC) **8**, 381
Chinese Art and Buddhism (AA) **22**, 157

BIRLEY, Eric
Senators in the Emperor's Service **39**, 197
Sir Ian Archibald Richmond, 1902–65. Obituary **52**, 293

BLACK, The Very Revd. Matthew
(Revd.) Thomas Walter Manson, 1893–1958. Obituary **44**, 325
Paul Ernst Kahle, 1875–1965. Obituary **51**, 485

BLACK, R. D. Collison
(Sir) Ralph George Hawtrey, 1879–1975. Obituary **63**, 363

BLANSHARD, Brand
The Philosophy of Analysis (P) **38**, 39

BLOMFIELD, Sir REGINALD
The Tangled Skein. Art in England, 1800–1920 (AA) **9**, 375

BLUNDEN, Edmund
Romantic Poetry and the Fine Arts (W) **28**, 101

BLUNT, Anthony
Some Uses and Misuses of the Terms Baroque and Rococo as Applied to Architecture (AA) **58**, 215

BOAS, F. S.
Aspects of Classical Legend and History in Shakespeare. (S) **29**, 107

BODE, Carl
The Sound of American Literature a Century Ago. (STP) **47**, 97

BOLSOVER, G. H.
Robert William Seton-Watson, 1879–1951. Obituary **37**, 343

BONI, Giacomo
Trajan's Column **3**, 93

BORENIUS, Tancred
English Primitives (AA) **11**, 75

BOSANQUET, Bernard
The Meaning of Teleology **2**, 235

Edward Caird, 1835–1908. Obituary **3**, 379
Croce's Aesthetic **9**, 261

BOSCH-GIMPERA, P.
Two Celtic Waves in Spain (JR) **26**, 25

BOUTROUX, Émile
Certitude et Vérité (P) **6**, 481

BOWRA, Sir C. Maurice
John Dewar Denniston, 1887–1949. Obituary **35**, 219
Presidential Address, 8 July 1959 **45**, 17
Palladas and Christianity **45**, 255
Presidential Address, 6 July 1960 **46**, 29
Presidential Address, 5 July 1961 **47**, 27
Presidential Address, 11 July 1962 **48**, 31

BOXER, C. R.
Edgar Prestage, 1869–1951. Obituary **44**, 199
The Colour Question in the Portuguese Empire, 1415–1825 (R) **47**, 113

BRADBROOK, M. C.
Shakespeare's Primitive Art (S) **51**, 215

BRADBURY, Malcolm
The Outland Dart: American Writers and European Modernism (STP) **63**, 33

BRADLEY, A. C.
Coriolanus (S) **5**, 457
Bernard Bosanquet, 1848–1923. Obituary **10**, 563

BRADLEY, Henry
On the Relations between Spoken and Written Language, with special reference to English **6**, 211
The Numbered Lections in Old English Poetical MSS **7**, 165
Sir James Murray, 1837–1915. Obituary **8**, 545
On the Text of Abbo of Fleury's *Quaestiones Grammaticales* **10**, 181

BRAITHWAITE, R. B.
Moral Principles and Inductive Policies (P) **36**, 51
George Edward Moore, 1873–1958. Obituary **47**, 293
BRANDL, Alois
Shakespeare and Germany (S) **6**, 249
BREWER, Derek
Towards a Chaucerian Poetic (IG) **60**, 219
BRIDGE, Sir Frederick
Milton and Music **3**, 349
BROAD, C. D.
Sir Isaac Newton (MM) **13**, 173
John McTaggart Ellis McTaggart, 1866–1925. Obituary **13**, 307
William Ernest Johnson, 1858–1931. Obituary **17**, 491
Berkeley's Argument about Material Substance (P) **28**, 119
(Revd.) Frederick Robert Tennant, 1866–1957. Obituary **44**, 241
Hume's Doctrine of Space (DH) **47**, 161
BROCKBANK, Philip
'Upon Such Sacrifices' (S) **62**, 109
BROGAN, Sir Denis
The Debate on the American Civil War (STP) **49**, 203
BROOKE, C. N. L.
(Revd.) David Knowles, 1896–1974. Obituary **61**, 439
BROOKE, Nicholas
Shakespeare and Baroque Art (S) **63**, 53
BROOKE, Z. N.
Lay Investiture and its Relation to the Conflict of Empire and Papacy (R) **25**, 217
BROOKNER, Anita
Jacques-Louis David: A Personal Interpretation (AA) **60**, 155
BROWN, Sir Henry Phelps
The Trade Union and the Common Weal (TOB) **53**, 165
Sir Alexander Morris Carr-Saunders, 1886–1966. Obituary **53**, 379

BROWN, Julian
Francis Wormald, 1904–72. Obituary **61**, 523
BROWN, P. Hume
Andrew Lang, 1844–1912. Obituary **5**, 552
BROWNE, Edward G.
The Persian Constitutional Movement **8**, 311
BRYCE, Viscount
Presidential Address, 10 July 1914 **6**, 7
Presidential Address at the Opening Meeting of the International Congress of Historical Studies, 3 April 1913 **6**, 121
Presidential Address, 30 June 1915 **7**, 1
Presidential Address, 14 July 1916 **7**, 17
Presidential Address: The Next Thirty Years, 19 July 1917 **8**, 1
World History (R) **9**, 187
Lord Reay, 1839–1921. Obituary **10**, 533
BUCHAN, John
Lord Rosebery, 1847–1929. Obituary **16**, 392
BUCHTAL, Hugo
The Western Aspects of Gandhara Sculpture (AA) **31**, 151
BUENO DE MESQUITA, D. M.
Some Condottieri of the Trecento (I) **32**, 219
BULLOCK, Alan (Lord Bullock)
Hitler and the Origins of the Second World War (R) **53**, 259
BULLOUGH, Geoffrey
Changing Views of the Mind in English Poetry (W) **41**, 61
Shakespeare, the Elizabethan (S) **50**, 121
BURKITT, F. C.
The Syriac Forms of New Testament Proper Names **5**, 377
The Early Syriac Lectionary System **10**, 301
Robert Henry Charles, 1855–1931. Obituary **17**, 437

BURNET, John
The Socratic Doctrine of the Soul
(P) **7**, 235
Aristotle (MM) **11**, 109
BURROW, Thomas
Herbert Neil Randle, 1880–1973.
Obituary **60**, 431
BURY, J. B.
The Imperial Administrative System
in the Ninth Century **4**, 347
BUTCHER, S. H.
President's Address at the Eighth
Annual General Meeting, 28 June
1910 **4**, 9
Presidential Address: Tennyson
4, 21
BUTLER, Lionel
E. H. W. Meyerstein, 1889–1952
(C) **41**, 141
BUTLER, Rohan
Sir Llewellyn Woodward, 1890–
1971. Obituary **57**, 497
BUTT, John E.
Pope's Poetical Manuscripts (W)
40, 23
James Blair Leishman, 1902–63.
Obituary **49**, 459
BUTTERFIELD, Sir Herbert
George Peabody Gooch, 1873–1968.
Obituary **55**, 311
Sincerity and Insincerity in Charles
James Fox (R) **57**, 237
BUXTON, John
The Poetry of Lord Byron (W)
56, 77

C

CAIRD, Edward
Idealism and the Theory of Know-
ledge **1**, 95
CAIRD, Revd. George B.
(Revd.) Charles Harold Dodd,
1884–1973. Obituary **60**, 497
CALDER, Sir W. M.
William Hepburn Buckler, 1867–
1952. Obituary **40**, 275

CALLUS, D. A.
Introduction of Aristotelian Learn-
ing to Oxford **29**, 229
CAM, Helen M.
The Legislators of Medieval Eng-
land (R) **31**, 127
Zachary Nugent Brooke, 1883–
1946. Obituary **32**, 381
CAMERON, Kenneth
The significance of English Place-
Names (IG) **62**, 135
CAMPBELL, A. H.
Obligation and Obedience to Law
(Mac) **51**, 337
CAMPBELL, C. A.
Moral Intuition and the Principle
of Self-Realisation (P) **34**, 23
CAPPER, J. B.
Andrew Seth Pringle-Pattison,
1856–1931. Obituary **17**, 447
CARR, Sir Cecil
George James Turner, 1867–1946.
Obituary **40**, 207
CARR, E. H.
The Russian Revolution and the
Peasant (R) **49**, 69
CARR, H. Wildon
'Time' and 'History' in Contem-
porary Philosophy; with special
reference to Bergson and Croce
8, 331
CARRITT, E. F.
An Ambiguity of the Word 'Good'
(P) **23**, 51
Benedetto Croce, 1866–1952. Obit-
uary **38**, 345
CARSON, R. A. G.
Harold Mattingly, 1884–1964.
Obituary **50**, 331
CARTER, Hazel
Malcolm Guthrie, 1903–72. Obit-
uary **59**, 473
CASEY, John
T. S. Eliot: Language, Sincerity,
and the Self (C) **63**, 95
CATLIN, George E. Gordon
(Sir) Ernest Barker, 1874–1960.
Obituary **46**, 341

CATON-THOMPSON, Gertrude
Dorothy Annie Elizabeth Garrod, 1892–1968. Obituary **55**, 339
CECIL, Lord David
The Poetry of Thomas Gray (W) **31**, 43
ČERNÝ, Jaroslav
Sir Alan Gardiner, 1879–1963. Obituary **50**, 263
CERULLI, E.
Tiberius and Pontius Pilate in Ethiopian Tradition and Poetry **59**, 141
CHADWICK, Norah K.
The Colonization of Brittany from Celtic Britain (JR) **51**, 235
CHALMERS, Lord
Thomas William Rhys Davids, 1843–1922. Obituary **10**, 540
CHAMBERS, Sir Edmund K.
The Disintegration of Shakespeare (S) **11**, 89
Matthew Arnold (W) **18**, 23
CHAMBERS, R. W.
W. P. Ker, 1855–1923. Obituary **11**, 413
The Saga and the Myth of Sir Thomas More (LH) **12**, 179
Bede (MM) **22**, 129
The Jacobean Shakespeare and *Measure for Measure* (S) **23**, 135
Poets and their Critics: Langland and Milton(W) **27**, 109
CHARLES, The Revd. Canon R. H.
An Attempt to Recover the Original Order of the Text of Revelation xx.4–xxii **7**, 37
Thomas Kelly Cheyne, 1841–1915. Obituary **7**, 545
CHARLESWORTH, Revd. M. P.
The Virtues of a Roman Emperor (R) **23**, 105
CHARLTON, H. B.
'Romeo and Juliet' as an Experimental Tragedy (S) **25**, 143
CHENEY, C. R.
Helen Maud Cam, 1885–1968. Obituary **55**, 293

CHESHIRE, Geoffrey
Cecil Herbert Stuart Fifoot, 1899–1975. Obituary **61**, 429
CHEYNEY, E. P.
Henry Charles Lea, 1825–1909. Obituary **5**, 517
CHILDE, V. Gordon
Henri Frankfort, 1897–1954. Obituary **41**, 367
CIPPICO, Antonio
The Poetry of Ugo Foscolo (I) **11**, 13
CLAPHAM, Sir A. W.
The Renaissance of Architecture and Stone-carving in Southern France in the Tenth and Eleventh Centuries (AA) **18**, 47
CLAPHAM, Sir John H.
William Robert Scott, 1868–1940. Obituary **26**, 479
Presidential Address, 9 July 1941 **27**, 19
Lord Stamp, 1880–1941. Obituary **27**, 453
Presidential Address, 15 July 1942 **28**, 13
Presidential Address, 14 July 1943 **29**, 13
William Arthur Shaw, 1865–1943. Obituary **29**, 349
Presidential Address, 12 July 1944 **30**, 13
Presidential Address, 11 July 1945 **31**, 13
CLARK, Albert C.
Robinson Ellis, 1834–1913. Obituary **6**, 517
F. C. Conybeare, 1856–1924. Obituary **11**, 469
James Smith Reid, 1846–1926. Obituary **13**, 335
Louis Claude Purser, 1854–1932. Obituary **18**, 407
CLARK, Sir George N.
The Birth of the Dutch Republic (R) **32**, 189
Sir John Harold Clapham, 1873–1946. Obituary **32**, 339

CLARK, Sir George N. (*cont.*):
Presidential Address, 6 July 1955
41, 15
Presidential Address, 4 July 1956
42, 17
Presidential Address, 10 July 1957
43, 17
Presidential Address, 9 July 1958
44, 15
Sir Charles Webster and the British Academy. Obituary **48**, 446
George Macauley Trevelyan, 1876–1962. Obituary **49**, 375
Sir David Ross, 1877–1971. Obituary **57**, 525

CLARK, Grahame
The Economic Approach to Prehistory (AR) **39**, 215
Osbert Guy Stanhope Crawford, 1886–1957. Obituary **44**, 281

CLARK, J. Desmond
Louis Seymour Bazett Leakey, 1903–72. Obituary **59**, 447

CLARK, Lord (Sir Kenneth Clark)
On the Painting of English Landscape (AA) **21**, 185
Leon Battista Alberti on Painting (I) **30**, 283

CLEMEN, Wolfgang
Past and Future in Shakespeare's Drama (S) **52**, 231

COBB, R. C.
Modern French History in Britain (R) **60**, 271

COBURN, Kathleen
The Interpretation of Man and Nature (W) **49**, 95

COGHILL, Nevill
The Pardon of Piers Plowman (IG) **30**, 303

COHEN, L. J.
Probability—The One and the Many (P) **61**, 83

COLGRAVE, Bertram
The Earliest Saints' Lives Written in England (IG) **44**, 35

COLLINGWOOD, R. G.
Human Nature and Human History **22**, 97

COLLINS, Arthur Jefferies
The Documents of the Great Charter of 1215 **34**, 233

CONWAY, R. Seymour
The Records of the Venetic Language **3**, 159
Sir William Ridgeway, 1853–1926. Obituary **12**, 327
Vergil's Creative Art (AA) **17**, 17

COOK, S. A.
(The Very Revd. Sir) George Adam Smith, 1856–1942. Obituary **28**, 325

COPLESTON, Revd. Frederick C.
Bergson on Morality (DH) **41**, 247

CORMACK, J. M. R.
(Sir) William Moir Calder, 1881–1960. Obituary **47**, 345

COULTON, G. G.
Some Problems in Medieval Historiography (R) **18**, 155

COURTHOPE, W. J.
A Consideration of Macaulay's Comparison of Dante & Milton **3**, 259
The Connection between Ancient and Modern Romance (W) **5**, 245

COWLEY, Sir Arthur E.
Samuel Rolles Driver, 1846–1914. Obituary **7**, 540
The Date of the Hittite Hieroglyphic Inscriptions of Carchemish **14**, 39

CRAIGIE, Sir William A.
The Scottish Alliterative Poems (IG) **28**, 217

CREED, Revd. J. M.
(The Very Revd.) Joseph Armitage Robinson, 1858–1933. Obituary **20**, 297

CRESWELL, Sir K. Archibald C.
Fortification in Islam before AD 1250 (AA) **38**, 89

CROCE, Benedetto
Recenti Controversie intorno all' unità della storia d'Italia (I) **22**, 57

CROFTS, J.
Wordsworth and the Seventeenth
Century (W)　　　26, 179
CROOK, John
Arnold Hugh Martin Jones, 1904–
70. Obituary　　　57, 425
CROSS, J. E.
The Literate Anglo-Saxon (IG)
58, 67
CRUM, W. E.
Francis Llewellyn Griffith, 1862–
1934. Obituary　　　20, 309
Coptic Documents in Greek Script
25, 249
CUNNINGHAM, The Ven. W.
Notes on the Organisation of the
Masons' Craft in England 6, 167
CURLE, A. O.
Sir George Macdonald, 1862–1940.
Obituary　　　27, 433

D

DAICHES, David
Sir Herbert Grierson, 1866–1960.
Obituary　　　46, 319
Literature and Education in the
United States (STP)　　　51, 357
DALTON, O. M.
The Byzantine Astrolabe at Brescia
12, 133
Sir Hercules Read, 1857–1929.
Obituary　　　15, 519
DANIEL, Glyn E.
Who are the Welsh? (JR)　40, 145
DARBISHIRE, Helen
Ernest de Selincourt, 1870–1943.
Obituary　　　29, 393
DAVID, Richard W.
Shakespeare and the Players (S)
47, 139
DAVIDS, T. W. Rhys
Oriental Studies in England and
Abroad　　　1, 183
Edward Byles Cowell. Obituary
1, 302
Cosmic Law in Ancient Thought
8, 279

DAVIE, Donald
The Poetry of Sir Walter Scott (C)
47, 61
DAVIES, Godfrey
(Sir) Charles Harding Firth 1857–
1936. Obituary　　　22, 380
DAVIES, K. G.
The End of British Administration
in the North American Colonies
(STP)　　　61, 131
DAVIS, Herbert J.
Frank Percy Wilson, 1889–1963.
Obituary　　　49, 441
DAVIS, H. W. C.
The Great Game in Asia (1800–
44) (R)　　　12, 227
DAVIS, Norman
The Language of the Pastons (IG)
40, 119
DAWKINS, R. M.
Peter Giles, 1860–1935. Obituary
21, 406
DAWSON, Christopher
Edward Gibbon (MM)　20, 159
DAWSON, Warren R.
Battiscombe George Gunn, 1883–
1950. Obituary　　　36, 229
DE BEER, Sir Gavin
Charles Darwin (MM)　44, 163
DE BILDT, Baron
The Conclave of Clement X (1670)
1, 111
DE BURGH, W. G.
The Relations of Morality to
Religion (P)　　　21, 75
George Dawes Hicks, 1862–1941.
Obituary　　　27, 405
DE FILIPPI, Lt. Col. Sir Filippo
Italy's Protection of Art Treasures
and Monuments during the War
(I)　　　8, 291
The Relations of the House of
Savoy with the Court of England
8, 447
DE LA MARE, Walter
Poetry in Prose (W)　　21, 239
DELARGY J. H.
The Gaelic Story-teller (JR)
31, 177

DELEHAYE, Pére Hippolyte
'In Britannia' dans le Martyrologe
Hiéronymien   **17**, 289
DE NAVARRO, J. M.
A Survey of Research on an Early
Phase of Celtic Culture (JR)
                              22, 297
Hector Munro Chadwick, 1870–
1947. Obituary   **33**, 307
DENHOLM-YOUNG, N.
The Song of Carlaverock and the
Parliamentary Roll of Arms
                              47, 251
DENT, Edward J.
Music of the Renaissance in Italy
(I)   **19**, 293
Mozart (MM)   **39**, 181
D' ENTRÈVES, A. P.
Alessandro Manzoni (I)   **36**, 23
DE REYNOLD, G.
Comment se forme une nation: la
Suisse, sa terre et son histoire
                              8, 419
DE SÉLINCOURT, Ernest
Keats (W)   **10**, 59
DEVLIN, Lord (Hon. Sir Patrick
Devlin)
The Enforcement of Morals (Mac)
                              45, 129
DICKINS, Bruce
J. M. Kemble and Old English
Scholarship (IG)   **25**, 51
DILLON, Myles
The Archaism of Irish Tradition
(JR)   **33**, 245
DIONISOTTI, Carlo
Manzoni and the Catholic Revival
(I)   **59**, 341
DIXON, W. Macneile
Chatterton (W)   **16**, 183
DOBRÉE, Bonamy
The Theme of Patriotism in the
Poetry of the Early Eighteenth
Century (W)   **35**, 49
DOBSON, E. J.
The Date and Composition of
Ancrene Wisse (IG)   **52**, 181

DODD, Revd. C. H.
(Revd.) Wilfred Lawrence Knox,
1886–1950. Obituary   **47**, 263
DOUGLAS, David C.
The Rise of Normandy (R)
                              33, 101
Alexander Hamilton Thompson,
1873–1952. Obituary   **38**, 317
DOVER, K. J.
William Laughton Lorimer, 1885–
1967. Obituary   **53**, 437
DOWDEN, Edward
Milton in the Eighteenth Century
(1701–1750)   **3**, 275
DRINKWATER, John
Some Contributions to the English
Anthology (W)   **10**, 181
DRIVER, Sir Godfrey R.
Reginald Campbell Thompson,
1876–1941. Obituary   **30**, 447
David Winton Thomas, 1901–70.
Obituary   **57**, 463
DRIVER, Revd. S. R.
Professor Davidson. Obituary
                              1, 289
DUFF, P. W.
William Warwick Buckland, 1859–
1946. Obituary   **33**, 283
DUMMETT, M. A. E.
The Justification of Deduction (P)
                              59, 201
DUNBABIN, T. J.
Sir John Myres, 1869–1954. Obit-
uary.   **41**, 349
DUNCAN, G. A.
Charles Francis Bastable, 1855–
1945. Obituary   **31**, 241
DUNCAN-JONES, Elsie
Marvell: A Great Master of Words
(W)   **61**, 267
DUNEDIN, Viscount
Richard Burdon Haldane, 1856–
1928. Obituary   **14**, 405
DYSON, H. V. D.
The Emergence of Shakespeare's
Tragedy (S)   **36**, 69

E

EDWARDS, I. E. S.
Stephen Ranulph Kingdon Glanville, 1900–1956. Obituary
44, 231
Jaroslav Černý, 1898–1970. Obituary **58**, 367

EDWARDS, Sir J. Goronwy
Edward I's Castle-Building in Wales (JR) **32**, 15
Sir John Edward Lloyd, 1861–1947. Obituary **41**, 319
The Normans and the Welsh March (R) **42**, 155

EDWARDS, Philip
Person and Office in Shakespeare's Plays (S) **56**, 93

EHRENPREIS, Irvin
Jonathan Swift (MM) **54**, 149

ELIOT, T. S.
Milton (MM) **33**, 61

ELLIOT, J. H.
The Discovery of America and the Discovery of Man (R) **58**, 101

ELLIS-FERMOR, Una
Shakespeare the Dramatist (S) **34**, 81

ELTON, G. R.
Reform by Statute: Thomas Starkie's *Dialogue* & Thomas Cromwell's Policy (R) **54**, 165

ELTON, Oliver
Poetic Romances after 1850 (W) **6**, 413
George Edward Bateman Saintsbury, 1845–1933. Obituary **19**, 325
Style in Shakespeare (S) **22**, 69
Lascelles Abercrombie, 1881–1938. Obituary **25**, 394

ELY, Bishop of
see WYNN

EMERSON, O. F.
John Dryden and a British Academy **10**, 45

EMERTON, J. A.
(Sir) Godfrey Rolles Driver, 1892–1975. Obituary **63**, 345

EMERY, W. B.
Aylward Manley Blackman, 1883–1956. Obituary **44**, 225

EMMETT, Dorothy
Alfred North Whitehead, 1861–1947. Obituary **33**, 293
Presuppositions and Finite Truths (P) **35**, 67

ENTHOVEN, R. E.
Sir Richard Temple, Bt., 1850–1931. Obituary. (signed E. R. E.) **17**, 393

EVANS, Sir Arthur J.
The Pictographic and Linear Scripts of Minoan Crete and their Relations **1**, 137

EVANS, Sir David L.
Sir Cyril Flower, 1879–1961. Obituary **48**, 387

EVERETT, Barbara
Donne: a London Poet (C) **58**, 245

EVERETT, Dorothy
Some Reflections on Chaucer's 'Art Poetical' (IG) **36**, 131

EVERSHED, Lord
The Impact of Statute on the Law of England (Mac) **42**, 247

EWERT, Alfred
William James Entwistle, 1895–1952. Obituary **38**, 333
John Orr, 1885–1966. Obituary **52**, 323

EWING, A. C.
Reason and Intuition (P) **27**, 67
Norman Kemp Smith, 1872–1958. Obituary **45**, 297

F

FARNELL, L. R.
The Value and the Methods of Mythologic Study **9**, 37
Hedonism and Art **14**, 99

FFOULKES, C.
Viscount Dillon, 1844–1932. Obituary **18**, 335

FIELD, G. C.
Some Problems of the Philosophy of History (P) **24**, 55

FINDLAY, J. N.
The Structure of the Kingdom of
Ends (P)   **43**, 97
FINLEY, M. I.
Schliemann's Troy—One Hundred
Years After (MW)   **60**, 393
FIRTH, Sir Charles H.
Dr S. R. Gardiner. Obituary
                             1, 295
Milton as an Historian   **3**, 227
The Study of Modern History in
Great Britain considered in con-
nection with Education, the Or-
ganization of the Archives, and
the Documentary Publications of
the Government   **6**, 139
Sir Walter Raleigh's History of the
World   **8**, 427
The Political Significance of 'Gul-
liver's Travels'   **9**, 237
Sir Sidney Lee, 1859–1926. Obit-
uary   **15**, 445
Joseph Wright, 1855–1930. Obit-
uary   **18**, 423
FIRTH, Sir Raymond W.
Alfred Reginald Radcliffe-Brown,
1881–1955. Obituary   **42**, 287
The Sceptical Anthropologist? Social
Anthropology and Marxist Views
on Society (RB)   **58**, 177
Max Gluckman, 1911–75. Obituary
                            61, 479
FISHER, H. A. L.
Viscount Bryce of Dechmont, 1838–
1922. Obituary   **12**, 297
The Whig Historians (R) **14**, 297
Presidential Address, 13 July 1932
                            18, 15
FITZMAURICE-KELLY, James
Cervantes in England   **2**, 11
Cervantes and Shakespeare (MM)
                             7, 297
FLEURE, H. J.
Archaeology and Folk Tradition
(JR)   **17**, 369
FLOWER, Robin
Ireland and Medieval Europe (JR)
                            13, 271

Laurence Nowell and the Discovery
of England in Tudor Times (IG)
                            21, 47
FOLIGNO, Cesare
Dante—the Poet (I)   **10**, 81
Edmund Garratt Gardner, 1869–
1935. Obituary   **21**, 464
FOOT, Philippa
Morality and Art (P)   **56**, 131
FORSDYKE, E. J.
Minoan Art (AA)   **15**, 45
FORTES, Meyer
Cyril Daryll Forde, 1902–73. Obit-
uary   **62**, 459
FORTESCUE, The Hon. Sir John
The British Soldier and the Empire
(R)   **9**, 409
FOSTER, Idris Ll.
The Book of the Anchorite (JR)
                            36, 197
Sir Ifor Williams, 1881–1965. Obit-
uary   **53**, 361
FOSTER, Kenelm
The Idea of Truth in Manzoni and
Leopardi (I)   **53**, 243
FOX, Sir Cyril
The Boundary Line of Cymru (JR)
                            26, 275
FRAENKEL, Eduard
Horace   **22**, 31
Aeschylus: New Texts and Old
Problems   **28**, 237
FRANCIS, Sir Frank
Victor Scholderer, 1880–1971.
                            58, 429
FRANK, Tenney
Cicero (MM)   **18**, 111
FRASER, A. Campbell
John Locke as a Factor in Modern
Thought   **1**, 221
FRASER, G. S.
Keith Douglas: A Poet of the Second
World War (C)   **42**, 89
FRASER, J.
Linguistic Evidence and Archaeo-
logical and Ethnological Facts
(JR)   **12**, 257

FRASER, P. M.
   Some Alexandrian Forgeries
                              47, 243
   Eratosthenes of Cyrene (MM)
                              56, 175
FRAZER, Sir J. G.
   Jacob and the Mandrakes   8, 57
FRY, Sir Edward
   The Rights of Neutrals, as illustrated
      by Recent Events   2, 265
FULLER, John
   Carving Trifles: William King's
      Imitation of Horace (C)   62, 269

G

GADD, C. J.
   The Fall of Nineveh   10, 473
   Seals of Ancient Indian Style found
      at Ur   18, 191
   Stephen Herbert Langdon, 1876–
      1937. Obituary   23, 565
GALBRAITH, V. H.
   The Literacy of the Medieval Eng-
      lish Kings (R)   21, 201
   Albert Frederick Pollard, 1869–
      1948. Obituary   35, 257
   Austin Lane Poole, 1889–1963.
      Obituary   49, 431
   A Draft of Magna Carta (1215)
                              53, 345
GARDINER, Sir Alan H.
   Some Aspects of the Egyptian Lan-
      guage   23, 81
GARDINER, Patrick
   Kierkegaard's Two Ways (DH)
                              54, 207
GARDNER, Edmund G.
   Dante (MM)   10, 97
   Notes on the 'Matière de Bretagne'
      in Italy   15, 179
   Virgil in Italian Poetry (I) 17, 75
   Paget Toynbee, 1855–1932. Obit-
      uary   18, 441
GARDNER, Dame Helen L.
   The Noble Moor (S)   41, 189
   Clive Staples Lewis, 1898–1963.
      Obituary   51, 417

   Herbert John Davis, 1893–1967.
      Obituary   54, 289
GARDNER, Percy
   Psychological Elements in Greek
      Sculpture   1, 251
   The Gold Coinage of Asia before
      Alexander the Great   3, 107
   The Earliest Coins of Greece Proper
                              5, 161
GARROD, Dorothy A. E.
   The Natufian Culture (AR)
                              43, 211
GARROD, H. W.
   The Poetry of Collins (W)   14, 21
   Percy Stafford Allen, 1869–1933.
      Obituary   19, 381
   David Ansell Slater, 1866–1938.
      Obituary   25, 339
GASELEE, Sir Stephen
   Montague Rhodes James, 1862–
      1936. Obituary   22, 418
GEACH, P. T.
   Some Problems about Time (P)
                              51, 321
GEACH, Mrs P. T.
   see Anscombe, G. E. M.
GETTY, Robert J.
   Alexander Souter, 1873–1949. Obit-
      uary.   38, 255
GIBSON, James
   John Locke (MM)   19, 29
GILSON, Étienne
   Saint Thomas Aquinas (MM)
                              21, 29
GIRVAN, Ritchie
   Finnsburuh (IG)   26, 327
GLOVER, T. R.
   The Mind of St. Paul (MM)
                              27, 247
GLUCKMAN, Max
   African Traditional Law in Histori-
      cal Perspective (RB)   60, 295
GODFREY, Walter H.
   Sir Alfred Clapham, 1883–1950.
      Obituary   39, 351
GOLLANCZ, Sir Israel
   Shakesperiana, 1598–1602   1, 199
   Spenseriana   3, 99

GOLLANCZ, Sir Israel (*cont.*):
Address to the Hebrew University
of Jerusalem　　　　　　11, 11
GOMBRICH, Sir Ernst H.
Lessing (MM)　　　　　43, 133
GOOCH, G. P.
John George Robertson, 1867–1933.
Obituary　　　　　　19, 360
Hobbes (MM)　　　　　25, 85
Harold Temperley, 1879–1939.
Obituary　　　　　　25, 355
GOODHART, A. L.
Lord Wright, 1869–1964. Obituary
　　　　　　　　　51, 429
Sir Carleton Kemp Allen, 1887–
1966. Obituary　　　53, 391
GOODMAN, Lord
Erosions of Personal Freedom in a
Modern Society (TOB)　54, 133
GOODWIN, A.
Revd. James Matthew Thomp-
son, 1878–1956. Obituary
　　　　　　　　　43, 271
GORDON, George
Shelley and the Oppressors of Man-
kind (W)　　　　　10, 257
Virgil in English Poetry (W)
　　　　　　　　　17, 39
GOSSE, Sir Edmund
Two Pioneers of Romanticism:
Joseph and Thomas Warton (W)
　　　　　　　　　7, 145
GOW, A. S. F.
Sir Stephen Gaselee, KCMG, 1882–
1943. Obituary　　　29, 441
GOWING, Margaret
Richard Morris Titmuss, 1907–73.
Obituary　　　　　　61, 401
GRANT, Douglas
Nationalism and the Literature of
the United States (STP)　53, 179
GRANVILLE-BARKER, Harley
From Henry V to Hamlet (S)
　　　　　　　　　11, 283
GRAYSON, Cecil
Leon Battista Alberti and the
Beginnings of Italian Grammar
(I)　　　　　　　　49, 291

GREG, Sir W. W.
Principles of Emendation in Shake-
speare (S)　　　　　14, 147
Ronald Brunlees McKerrow, 1872–
1940. Obituary　　　26, 489
GRICE, G. R.
Alfred Cyril Ewing, 1899–1973.
Obituary　　　　　　59, 499
GRICE, H. P.
Intention and Uncertainty (P)
　　　　　　　　　57, 263
GRIERSON, Sir H. J. C.
Lord Byron: Arnold and Swin-
burne (W)　　　　　9, 431
Thomas Carlyle (MM)　26, 301
GRIFFITH, F. Ll.
Christian Documents from Nubia
　　　　　　　　　14, 117
GRISWOLD, Erwin N.
Two branches of the Same Stream
(Mac)　　　　　　　48, 235
GRIVELET, Michel
A Portrait of the Artist as Proteus
(S)　　　　　　　　61, 153
GUNN, Battiscombe
Walter Ewing Crum, 1865–1944.
Obituary　　　　　　34, 281
GURNEY, Oliver R.
The Assyrian Tablets from Sultan-
tepe　　　　　　　　41, 21

H

HACKING, Ian
Leibnitz and Descartes: Proof and
Eternal Truths (DH)　59, 175
HADOW, Sir W. Henry
Beethoven (MM)　　　8, 135
William Byrd (AA)　　10, 395
HAKE, Henry M.
The English Historic Portrait: Docu-
ment and Myth (AA)　29, 133
HALDANE, Viscount
The Doctrine of Degrees in Know-
ledge, Truth and Reality　9, 109
Bernard Bosanquet, 1848–1923.
Obituary　　　　　　10, 563
Address to the Hebrew University
of Jerusalem　　　　11, 11

HAMEL, A. G. van
Aspects of Celtic Mythology (JR)
20, 207
HAMILTON, R. W.
(Sir) Keppel Archibald Cameron
Cresswell, 1879–1974. Obituary
60, 459
HAMMOND, N. G. L.
(Sir) Frank Ezra Adcock, 1886–
1968. Obituary 54, 425
HAMPSHIRE, Stuart
Spinoza and the Idea of Freedom
(P) 46, 195
Friederich Waismann, 1896–1959.
Obituary 46, 309
HANBURY, Harold G.
Robert Warden Lee, 1868–1958.
Obituary 44, 313
HANCOCK, W. K.
A lonely Patriot: Ferdinando Ra-
nalli (I) 27, 275
HARBAGE, Alfred
Shakespeare without Words (S)
55, 129
HARDIE, W. F. R.
Naturalistic Ethics (P) 33, 29
HARE, R. M.
Descriptivism (P) 49, 115
HARRIS, J. Rendel
F. C. Conybeare, 1856–1924. Obit-
uary 11, 469
HART, H. L. A.
Bentham (MM) 48, 297
HART, H. St. John
Norman McLean, 1865–1947. Obit-
uary 63, 399
HAVERFIELD, F. J.
The Romanization of Roman Bri-
tain 2, 185
Henry Francis Pelham, 1846–1907.
Obituary 3, 365
First Report on Recent Excavations
in Roman Britain 4, 319
Report of Discoveries of Roman
Remains in Britain in 1912
5, 409
HAWKES, Christopher F. C.
Britain and Julius Caesar (MW)
63, 125

HAWKES, Jacquetta
(Sir) Robert Eric Mortimer Wheeler
1890–1976. Obituary, 63, 483
HAY, Denys
Flavio Biondo and the Middle Ages
(I) 45, 97
HAYEK, F. A.
Rules, Perception, and Intelligibility
48, 321
Dr Bernard Mandeville (MM)
52, 125
HAZELTINE, H. D.
Courtney Stanhope Kenny, 1847–
1930. Obituary 18, 345
Felix Liebermann, 1851–1925.
Obituary 24, 319
Sir Frederick Pollock, Bart, 1845–
1937. Obituary 35, 233
HEADLAM, M. F.
Sir Thomas Little Heath, 1861–
1940. Obituary 26, 425
HEANEY, Seamus
The Fire i' the Flint: Reflections
on the Poetry of Gerard Manley
Hopkins (C) 60, 413
HEARNSHAW, L. S.
(Sir) Cyril Lodowic Burt, 1883–
1971. Obituary 58, 475
HENN, T. R.
W. B. Yeats and the Poetry of War
(W) 51, 301
HERFORD, C. H.
Is there a Poetic View of the World?
(W) 7, 423
HESSE, Mary B.
In Defence of Objectivity (P)
58, 275
HICKS, G. Dawes
Shadworth Holloway Hodgson,
1832–1913. Obituary 6, 508
HICKS, Sir John
(Sir) Dennis Holme Robertson,
1890–1963. Obituary 50, 305
HILL, Sir George F.
Some Palestinian Cults in the
Graeco-Roman Age 5, 411
The Ancient Coinage of Southern
Arabia 7, 57

HILL, Sir George F. (*cont.*):
Italian Portraiture of the Fifteenth
  Century (I)   **11**, 331
Treasure-Trove—The Law and
  Practice of Antiquity   **19**, 219
Percy Gardner, 1846–1937. Obit-
  uary   **23**, 459
The Medal: Its Place in Art (AA)
                           27, 225
Ormonde Maddock Dalton, 1866–
  1945. Obituary   **31**, 357
HIND, A. M.
Early Italian Engraving (AA)
                           16, 45
HODGKIN, Thomas
Ernst Curtius   **2**, 31
HODGSON, Phyllis
The Orcherd of Syon and the
  English Mystical Tradition (IG)
                           50, 229
HODGSON, Shadworth H
The Centenary of Kant's Death
                           1, 169
Inter-relation of the Academical
  Sciences   **2**, 219
Some Cardinal Points in Know-
  ledge   **5**, 28
HØEG, Carsten
The Oldest Slavonic Tradition of
  Byzantine Music   **39**, 37
HOGARTH, D. G.
Artemis Ephesia   **2**, 375
Hittite Problems and the Excava-
  tion of Carchemish   **5**, 361
Rostovtzeff's *Iranians and Greeks*
                           10, 356
George Nathaniel Curzon, Marquis
  Curzon of Kedleston, 1859–1925.
  Obituary   **11**, 502
HOLDSWORTH, Sir W. S.
Sir Paul Vinogradoff, 1854–1925.
  Obituary   **11**, 486
Sir Thomas Erskine Holland, 1835–
  1926. Obituary   **12**, 317
HOLLAND, Sir Thomas Erskine
Neutral Duties in a Maritime War
  as Illustrated by Recent Events,
                           2, 55

Proposed Changes in Naval Prize
  Law   **5**, 144
Lord Justice Kennedy, 1846–1915.
  Obituary   **7**, 552
HOLLOND, H. A.
Harold Dexter Hazeltine, 1871–
  1960. Obituary   **47**, 311
(Sir) Cecil Thomas Carr, 1878–
  1966. Obituary   **52**, 311
HOLLOWAY, John
Skelton (C)   **44**, 83
HOLMES, Sir C. J.
Leonardo da Vinci (MM)   **9**, 53
HOLT, J. C.
The End of the Anglo-Norman
  Realm (R)   **61**, 223
HOUGH, Graham
Free Verse (W)   **43**, 157
HOURANI, Albert
Sir Hamilton Gibb, 1895–1971.
  Obituary   **58**, 493
HUGHES, A. M. D.
The Theology of Shelley (W)
                          24, 191
HUGHES, Kathleen
The Welsh Latin Chronicles:
  Annales Cambriae and Related
  Texts (JR)   **59**, 233
HUMPHREYS, A. R.
Shakespeare's Histories and 'The
  Emotion of Multitude' (S)
                          54, 265
HUMPHREYS, R. A.
British Merchants and South Ameri-
  can Independence (R)   **51**, 151
HUNT, Arthur S.
B. P. Grenfell, 1869–1926. Obituary
                          12, 357
A Greek Cryptogram   **15**, 127
HUNTER, G. K.
Othello and Colour Prejudice (S)
                          53, 139
HURSTFIELD, Joel
(Sir) John Ernest Neale, 1890–1975.
  Obituary   **63**, 403
HUSSEY, J. M.
Norman Hepburn Baynes, 1877–
  1961. Obituary   **49**, 365

HUTTON, Edward
Some Aspects of the Genius of Giovanni Boccaccio (I) **10**, 219
HUTTON, W. H.
Edward Armstrong, 1846–1928. Obituary **14**, 395

I

ILBERT, Sir Courtenay P.
The Centenary of the French Civil Code **1**, 253
Lord Davey, 1833–1907. Obituary **3**, 371
Sir Alfred Lyall, 1835–1911. Obituary **5**, 525
INGE, The Very Revd. W. R.
Plotinus (MM) **15**, 19
ISAACS, J.
Shakespeare's Earliest Years in the Theatre (S) **39**, 119
ISHIGURO, Hidé
Pre-established Harmony *versus* Constant Conjunction (DH) **63**, 239

J

JACK, Ian
Robert Browning (W) **53**, 219
JACKSON, Kenneth
'Common Gaelic': The Evolution of the Goedelic Languages (JR) **37**, 71
Norah Kershaw Chadwick, 1891–1972. Obituary **58**, 537
JACKSON, W. W.
Ingram Bywater, 1840–1914. Obituary **7**, 521
Henry Fanshawe Tozer, 1829–1916. Obituary **7**, 566
JACOB, E. F.
Charles Bémont and his Services to English History **25**, 301
Reynold Pecock, Bishop of Chichester (R) **37**, 121
JACOBSTHAL, Paul
Imagery in Early Celtic Art (JR) **27**, 301

JAMES, D. G.
Wordsworth and Tennyson (W) **36**, 113
JAMISON, Evelyn
The Sicilian Norman Kingdom in the Mind of Anglo-Norman Contemporaries (I) **24**, 237
Judex Tarentinus **53**, 289
JEBB, Sir Richard C.
Bacchylides **1**, 203
Samson Agonistes and the Hellenic Drama **3**, 341
JEFFARES, A. Norman
Oliver St. John Gogarty (C) **46**, 73
JENKINS, Harold
Hamlet and Ophelia (S) **49**, 135
John Dover Wilson, 1881–1969. Obituary **59**, 383
JENKINS, R. J. H.
Richard MacGillivray Dawkins, 1871–1955. Obituary **41**, 373
JENKINS, Roy
British Foreign Policy since 1945 (TOB) **58**, 153
JENKS, C. Wilfred
Orthodoxy and Innovation in the Law of Nations (Mac) **57**, 215
JESPERSEN, Otto
Monosyllabism in English (E) **14**, 341
JESSOP, T. E.
Leon Roth, 1896–1963. Obituary **50**, 317
JOHNSON, Charles
Sir Henry Churchill Maxwell-Lyte, 1848–1940. Obituary **26**, 361
JOHNSON, H. C.
Charles Johnson, 1870–1961. Obituary **51**, 403
JOHNSTON, Arthur
The Poetry of William Collins (W) **59**, 321
JONES, A. H. M.
Michael Ivanovitch Rostovtzeff, 1870–1952. Obituary **38**, 347
JONES, Emrys
Pope and Dulness (C) **54**, 231

Jones, Gwyn
Egill Skallagrímsson in England
(IG)   38, 127
Jones, H. Stuart
A Flavian Relief in the Louvre
                       10, 358
Jones, Sir Henry
Tennyson   4, 131
Jones, John
Heathcote William Garrod, 1878–
1960. Obituary   48, 357
Jones, Thomas
The Black Book of Camarthen,
'Stanzas of the Graves' (JR)
                       53, 97
Jones, W. H. S.
'Hippocrates' and the *Corpus Hippo-
craticum*   31, 103
Joseph, H. W. B.
John Cook Wilson, 1849–1915.
Obituary   7, 555
A Comparison of Kant's Idealism
with that of Berkeley (P) 15, 213
Harold Henry Joachim, 1868–1938.
Obituary   24, 396
Jusserand, J. J.
'What to Expect of Shakespeare'
(S)   5, 223

K

Kahn, Lord
On Re-reading Keynes (K)
                       60, 361
Karageorghis, Vassos
Kition: Mycenaean and Phoenician
(MW)   59, 259
Keeling, S. V.
Descartes (MM)   34, 57
Kenny, A. J. P.
Mental Health in Plato's Republic
(DH)   55, 229
Arthur Norman Prior, 1914–69.
Obituary   56, 321
Kenyon, Sir Frederick G.
The Evidence of Greek Papyri with
regard to Textual Criticism
                       1, 139

Presidential Address. The Position
of an Academy in a Civilized
State, 4 July 1918   8, 37
Presidential Address, 3 July 1919
                       9, 1
Presidential Address. International
Scholarship, 21 July 1920 9, 21
Presidential Address. The Fellow-
ship of Learning, 6 July 1921
                       10, 3
Address to the Hebrew University
of Jerusalem   11, 11
Sir Edward Maunde Thompson,
1840–1929. Obituary   15, 477
Arthur James Balfour, 1848–1930.
Obituary   16, 410
Sir Israel Gollancz, 1863–1930.
Obituary   16, 424
Sir George Warner, 1845–1936.
Obituary   22, 345
The Western Text in the Gospels
and Acts   24, 287
Arthur Hamilton Smith, 1860–
1941. Obituary   27, 393
Ker, Neil
Kenneth Sisam, 1887–1971. Obit-
uary   58, 409
Ker, W. P.
On the History of the Ballads,
1100–1500   4, 179
Thomas Warton (W)   4, 349
Frederick James Furnival, 1825–
1910. Obituary   4, 375
Kermode, J. F.
Spenser and the Allegorists (W)
                       48, 261
Ketton-Cremer, R. W.
Lapidary Verse (W)   45, 237
Keynes, Lord (John Maynard Keynes)
Henry Somerton Foxwell, 1849–
1936. Obituary (signed J.M.K.)
                       23, 470
Keyser, K. L.
see Leyser K. J.
Kilpatrick, G. D.
A New Psalms Fragment 43, 229
Kinsley, Revd. James
Burns and the Peasantry, 1785 (W)
                       60, 135

KIRWAN, L. P.
Rome Beyond the Southern Egyptian Frontier (MW)   **63**, 13
KITTO, H. D. F.
Arnold Wycombe Gomme, 1886–1959. Obituary   **45**, 335
KLASENS, Adolf
Walter Bryan Emery, 1903–1971. Obituary   **58**, 379
KNEALE, W. C.
The Idea of Invention (P)   **41**, 85
Leonard James Russell, 1884–1971. Obituary   **57**, 513
KNIGHTS, L. C.
Shakespeare's Politics (S)   **43**, 115
KNOWLES, Revd. M. D.
C. W. Previté-Orton, 1877–1947. Obituary   **33**, 351
Archbishop Thomas Becket: A Character Study (R)   **35**, 177
The Censured Opinions of Uthred of Boldon   **37**, 305
Christopher Dawson, 1889–1970. Obituary   **57**, 439
William Abel Pantin, 1902–73. Obituary   **60**, 447
KNOX, T. M.
Robin George Collingwood, 1889–1943. Obituary   **29**, 469
KOESTLER, Arthur
The Lion and the Ostrich (TOB)   **59**, 189
KÖRNER, Stephan
Kant's Conception of Freedom (DH)   **53**, 193

L

LAIRD, John
Samuel Alexander, 1859–1938. Obituary (signed J. L.)   **24**, 378
The Limits of Speculative Humanism (P)   **26**, 149
LAITHWAITE, Sir Gilbert
The Marquess of Zetland, 1876–1961. Obituary   **47**, 387
LAMBERG-KARLOVSKY, C. C.
Urban Interaction on the Iranian Plateau: Excavations at Tepe Yahya, 1967–1973 (AR)   **59**, 283
LAMONT, Clare
The Poetry of the Early Waverley Novels (C)   **61**, 315
LANG, A.
The Origin of Terms of Human Relationship   **3**, 139
LANGDON, S. H.
Newly-Discovered Letters of Hammurabi   **10**, 357
LASCELLES, Mary M.
Robert William Chapman, 1881–1960. Obituary   **47**, 361
Shakespeare's Comic Insight (S)   **48**, 171
Geoffrey Tillotson, 1905–69. Obituary   **56**, 351
Robert Wyndham Ketton-Cremer, 1906–69. Obituary   **56**, 403
LEA, Kathleen
The Poetic Powers of Repitition (W)   **55**, 51
LEA, K. M.
(Revd.) Francis Ernest Hutchinson, 1871–1947. Obituary   **45**, 269
LEACH, Arthur F.
Milton as Schoolboy and Schoolmaster   **3**, 295
Some Results of Research in the History of Education in England; with Suggestions for its Continuance and Extension   **6**, 433
LEACH, Sir Edmund
Social Anthropology: A Natural Science of Society? (RB)   **62**, 157
LEE, R. W.
Hugo Grotius (MM)   **16**, 219
Edward Jenks, 1861–1939. Obituary   **26**, 399
Sir William Searle Holdsworth, 1871–1944. Obituary (signed R. W. L.)   **30**, 411
LEE, Sir Sidney
Shakespeare and the Italian Renaissance (S)   **7**, 122
LEECH, Clifford
Shakespeare's Tragic Fiction (S)   **59**, 159

LEFF, Gordon
John Wyclif: the Path to Dissent (R)
　　　　　　　　　　52, 143
LEGG, S. C. E.
Henry Julian White, 1859–1934.
Obituary　　　　　　22, 408
LEGOUIS, Émile
The Bacchic Element in Shake-
speare's Plays (S)　　12, 115
LEISHMAN, J. B.
Some Themes and Variations in the
Poetry of Andrew Marvell (W)
　　　　　　　　　　47, 223
LEPPARD, Raymond
Unexplored Relationships between
Early Seventeenth-Century Vene-
tian Opera and Contemporary
Music in France and England (I)
　　　　　　　　　　55, 99
LERNER, Lawrence
W. B. Yeats: Poet and Crank (C)
　　　　　　　　　　49, 49
LETHABY, W. R.
Medieval Paintings at Westminster
(AA)　　　　　　　13, 123
LEVY R.
Reynold Alleyne Nicholson, 1868–
1945. Obituary　　　31, 399
LEWIS, C. Day
The Lyrical Poetry of Thomas
Hardy (W)　　　　　37, 155
LEWIS, C. S.
Hamlet: The Prince or the Poem?
(S)　　　　　　　　28, 139
Hero and Leander (W)　38, 23
LEWIS, Henry
The Sentence in Welsh (JR) 28, 259
LEWY, C.
G. E. Moore on the Naturalistic
Fallacy (DH)　　　　50, 251
LEYSER, K. J. (wrongly printed as
Keyser, K. L.)
K. B. Macfarlane, 1903–66. Obit-
uary　　　　　　　62, 485
LITTLE, A. G.
Introduction of the Observant Friars
into England　　　　10, 455
Some recently discovered Franciscan
Documents and their relations to

the second Life of Celano and the
'Speculum Perfectionis'　12, 147
Charles Lethbridge Kingsford,
1862–1926. Obituary　12, 348
Roger Bacon (MM)　　14, 265
Introduction of the Observant
Friars into England: a Bull of
Alexander VI　　　　27, 155
An Illuminated Letter of Fraternity
　　　　　　　　　　27, 269
LIVINGSTONE, R. W.
Ruskin (MM)　　　　31, 85
LLOYD, A. C.
Activity and Description in Aristotle
and the Stoa (DH)　　56, 227
LLOYD, Sir John Edward
The Welsh Chronicles (JR) 14, 369
LLOYD, Seton H. F.
Bronze Age Architecture of Anatolia
(AR)　　　　　　　49, 153
LLOYD-JONES, Hugh
Sir Maurice Bowra, 1898–1971.
Obituary　　　　　　58, 393
LLOYD-JONES, J.
The Court Poets of the Welsh
Princes (JR)　　　　34, 167
LOBEL, E.
Cardinal Pole's Manuscripts 17, 97
The Medieval Latin 'Poetics'
　　　　　　　　　　17, 309
A Greek Historical Drama　35, 207
LONSDALE, Roger
The Poetry of Thomas Gray:
Versions of the Self (C)　59, 105
LORIMER, W. L.
John Burnet, 1863–1928. Obituary
　　　　　　　　　　14, 445
Herbert Jennings Rose, 1883–1961.
Obituary　　　　　　48, 397
LOT, Ferdinand
Bretons et Anglais aux Vme et VIme
Siècles (JR)　　　　16, 327
Low, Sidney
The Organisation of Imperial
Studies in London　　5, 491
LOWES, John Livingston
The Art of Geoffrey Chaucer (IG)
　　　　　　　　　　16, 297

LUCAS, F. L.
The Criticism of Poetry (W) **19**, 167
LUCE, A. A.
Immaterialism (P) **30**, 19
(The Most Revd.) Charles Frederick
D'Arcy, 1859–1938. Obituary
24, 361
LYALL, Sir A. C.
The Mogul Empire in relation to
the Modern History of Asia
2, 183
Sir Spencer Walpole, 1839–1907.
Obituary **3**, 373
LYALL, Sir Charles J.
Some Aspects of Ancient Arabic
Poetry; as illustrated by a little-
known Anthology **8**, 365
Transliteration of Arabic and Per-
sian. Report of the Committee
appointed by the Academy
8, 505

M

MABBOTT, J. D.
Moral Rules (P) **39**, 97
McBURNEY, C. B. M.
Early Man in the Soviet Union
(AR) **61**, 171
MacCALLUM, M. W.
The Dramatic Monologue in the
Victorian Period (W) **11**, 265
McCALLUM, R. B.
Robin George Collingwood, 1889–
1943. Obituary **29**, 463
MACDONALD, Sir George
P. Hume Brown, 1849–1918. Obit-
uary **8**, 591
The Silver Coinage of Crete, A
Metrological Note **9**, 289
Francis John Haverfield, 1860–
1919. Obituary **9**, 475
Gerard Baldwin Brown, 1849–1932.
Obituary **21**, 375
MACDONELL, A. A.
The Evolution of Ancient Indian
Architecture **4**, 29

MACE, C. A.
George Frederick Stout, 1860–1944.
Obituary **31**, 307
McFARLANE, K. B.
The Wars of the Roses (R) **50**, 87
McGREGOR, O. R. (Lord McGregor)
Family Breakdown and Social Policy
(Mac) **59**, 65
McINTOSH, Angus
Wulfstan's Prose (IG) **35**, 109
MACKAIL, J. W.
Shakespeare after Three Hundred
Years (S) **7**, 319
William John Courthope, 1842–
1917. Obituary **8**, 581
Bentley's Milton (W) **11**, 55
Virgil (MM) **17**, 55
Presidential Address, 12 July 1933
19, 19
Presidential Address, 11 July 1934
20, 17
Presidential Address, 10 July 1935
21, 19
Andrew Cecil Bradley, 1851–1935.
Obituary **21**, 385
Presidential Address, 1936 **22**, 21
McKERROW, Ronald B.
The Treatment of Shakespeare's
Text by his Earlier Editors, 1709–
1768 (S) **19**, 89
MACKIE, J. L.
What's Really Wrong with Pheno-
menalism? (P) **55**, 133
MACLAGAN, Sir Eric
A Romanesque Relief in York
Minster **10**, 479
The Appreciation of Sculpture (AA)
11, 311
McNAIR, Arnold D. (Lord McNair)
Alexander Pearce Higgins, 1865–
1935. Obituary **22**, 485
William Warwick Buckland, 1859–
1946. Obituary **33**, 283
(Sir) Hersch Lauterpacht, 1897–
1960. Obituary **47**, 371
McNEILL, William H.
Arnold Joseph Toynbee, 1889–
1975. Obituary **63**, 441

MACQUEEN, John
Alexander Scott and Scottish Court Poetry of the Middle Sixteenth Century (W)   **54**, 93
MAHOOD, Molly M.
Unblotted Lines: Shakespeare at Work (S)   **58**, 163
MAITLAND, F. W.
Sir Leslie Stephen. Obituary   **1**, 316
MAJOR, Kathleen
Doris Mary Stenton, 1894–1971. Obituary   **58**, 525
MALLOWAN, Sir Max
Elamite Problems (AR)   **55**, 255
Cyril John Gadd, 1893–1969. Obituary   **56**, 363
MANLY, J. M.
Chaucer and the Rhetoricians (W)   **12**, 95
MANN, Sir James G.
The Etched Decoration of Armour (AA)   **28**, 17
MARETT, R. R.
Lewis Richard Farnell, 1856–1934. Obituary   **20**, 285
Ferdinand Canning Scott Schiller, 1864–1937. Obituary   **23**, 538
(Sir) James George Frazer, 1854–1941. Obituary   **27**, 377
MARGOLIOUTH, D. S.
On Mahdis and Mahdism   **7**, 213
Two South Arabian Inscriptions   **11**, 177
On 'The Book of Religion and Empire' by 'Alī B. Rabban Al-Tabari   **16**, 165
MARINATOS, Spyridon
Life and Art in Prehistoric Thera (AR)   **57**, 351
MARSHALL, Geoffrey
John Petrov Plamenatz, 1912–75. Obituary   **62**, 419
MARTIN, L. C.
Thomas Warton and the Early Poems of Milton (W)   **20**, 25
Oliver Elton, 1861–1945. Obituary   **31**, 317

MASCALL, Revd. E. L.
(Revd.) Austin Marsden Farrer, 1904–68. Obituary   **54**, 435
MATHESON, P. E.
Lord Chalmers, 1858–1938. Obituary   **25**, 321
MATTHEWS, The Very Revd. W. R.
(The Very Revd.) William Ralph Inge, 1860–1954. Obituary   **40**, 263
MATTINGLY, H.
The Date of the Roman Denarius and other Landmarks in Early Roman Coinage   **18**, 211
The Imperial 'Vota'   **36**, 155
The Imperial 'Vota' (second Part)   **37**, 219
Some New Studies of the Roman Republican Coinage   **39**, 239
Roman Numismatics: Miscellaneous Notes   **43**, 179
Roman Numismatics: Further Miscellaneous Notes   **46**, 249
Various Numismatic Notes   **49**, 313
MAWER, Allen
English Place-Name Study   **10**, 31
MAXWELL, J. C.
Measure for Measure: The Play and the Themes (S)   **60**, 199
MAYNARD, Winifred
William Lindsay Renwick, 1889–1970. Obituary   **57**, 477
MEADE, J. E.
The Inheritance of Inequalities (K)   **59**, 355
MEEK, Ronald L.
Maurice Herbert Dobb, 1900–76. Obituary   **63**, 333
MEIGGS, Russell
Marcus Niebuhr Tod, 1878–1974. Obituary   **60**, 485
MEISS, Millard
The Master of the Breviary of Jean Sans Peur and the Limbourgs (AA)   **56**, 111
MELLAART, James
Çatal Hüyük, a Neolithic City in Anatolia (AR)   **51**, 201

MEREDITH, George
The Tercentenary of Milton's Birth:
Lines written in honour of the
occasion   3, 353

MEYER, Kuno
Whitley Stokes, 1830–1909. Obituary   4, 363

MILBURN, The Very Revd. Canon
R. L. P.
(Revd.) Robert Henry Lightfoot,
1883–1953. Obituary   40, 253

MILLER, Jonathan
Censorship and the Limits of Permission (TOB)   57, 281

MILNER, Viscount
George Joachim, First Viscount
Goschen, 1831–1907. Obituary
3, 359

MILSOM, S. F. C.
Theodore Frank Thomas Plucknett,
1897–1965. Obituary   51, 505

MINNS, Sir Ellis H.
The Art of the Northern Nomads
(AA)   28, 47

MITCHELL, Charles
Felice Feliciano *Antiquarius* (I)
47, 197

MITCHELL, Sir W.
The Quality of Life (P)   20, 249

MODRONE, Senator Visconti di
England and Italy—An Historical
Survey of a Great Friendship (I)
18, 135

MOMIGLIANO, Arnaldo
Cassiodorus and Italian Culture of
his Time (I)   41, 207

MORGAN, Edwin
Provenance and Problematics of
'Sublime and Alarming Images'
in Poetry (W)   63, 293

MORISON, J. L.
From Alexander Burnes to Frederick
Roberts (R)   22, 177

MORISON, Stanley
The Art of Printing (AA)   23, 373

MORRIS-JONES, Sir John
Sir John Rhŷs (JR)   11, 187

MUIR, Kenneth
Shakespeare and the Tragic Pattern
(S)   44, 145

MUIRHEAD, J. H.
John Stuart Mackenzie, 1860–1953.
Obituary   21, 433

MURE, G. R. G.
Some Elements in Hegel's Logic
(DH)   44, 21

MURRAY, Gilbert
Hamlet and Orestes: A Study in
Traditional Types (S)   6, 389
David Samuel Margoliouth, 1858–
1940. Obituary   26, 389
Herbert Albert Laurens Fisher
1865–1940. Obituary (signed G.
M.)   26, 455
Edwyn Robert Bevan, 1870–1943.
Obituary (signed G. M.)   29, 411
Francis Macdonald Comford, 1874–
1943. Obituary   29, 421

MURRAY, Sir James A. H.
William Richard Morfill, 1834–
1909. Obituary   4, 368

MYRES, Sir John L.
The Causes of the Break-up of the
Mycenean Régime in Cyprus
10, 355
John Knight Fotheringham, 1874–
1936. Obituary   23, 551
Sir Henry Stuart Jones, 1867–1939.
Obituary (signed J. L. M.)
26, 467
Sir Arthur Evans, 1851–1941. Obit-
uary   27, 323
The Structure of Stichomythia in
Attic Tragedy   34, 199

MYRES, J. N. L.
The Angles, the Saxons, and the
Jutes (R)   56, 145

N

NAMIER, Sir Lewis B.
1848: The Revolution of the Intel-
lectuals (R)   30, 161

NEALE, Sir John E.
The Elizabethan Political Scene (R)
34, 97

NEWBOLT, Sir Henry
Poetry and Time (W)   **8**, 487
NICHOLAS, H. G.
Violence in American Society (STP)
55, 145
(Sir) Denis William Brogan, 1900–
74. Obituary   **62**, 399
NICHOLSON, Reynold A.
Sir Charles James Lyall, 1845–1920.
Obituary   **9**, 492
NICOLL, Allardyce
Co-operation in Shakespearian
Scholarship (S)   **38**, 71
NOCK, A. D.
Magical Texts from a Bilingual
Papyrus in the British Museum
17, 235
NORWICH, Dean of
see Beeching
NOTESTEIN, Wallace
The Winning of the Initiative by the
House of Commons (R)   **11**, 125
NOWOTTNY, Winifred
'The Common Privileges of Poetry'
(W)   **52**, 61
NUNN, J. Percy
Anthropomorphism and Physics (P)
13, 13

O

OAKESHOTT, Walter F.
Cyril Bailey, 1871–1958. Obituary
46, 295
Egon Wellesz, 1885–1974. Obituary
61, 567
Ó CUÍV, Brian
Literary Creation and Irish Histori-
cal Tradition (JR)   **49**, 233
OLDHAM, C. E. A. W.
Sir Aurel Stein, 1862–1943. Obit-
uary   **29**, 329
OMAN, SIR Charles W. C.
Column and Line in the Peninsular
War   **4**, 321
O'RAHILLY, Thomas F.
The Goidels and their Predecessors
(JR)   **21**, 323

OTERO, Don M. Lopez
Architectural Commentary on the
Pharos of Alexandria   **19**, 277
OWEN, G. E. L.
The Platonism of Aristotle (DH)
51, 125
OWEN, S. G.
John Percival Postgate, 1853–1926.
Obituary   **12**, 337

P

PAGE, Sir Denys
Presidential Address, 12 July 1972
58, 61
Presidential Address, 11 July 1973
59, 57
Presidential Address, 10 July 1974
60, 129
PANTIN, W. A.
(Revd.) Herbert Edward Salter,
1863–1951. Obituary   **40**, 219
Ernest Fraser Jacob, 1894–1971.
Obituary   **58**, 447
PARES, Richard
Basil Williams, 1867–1950. Obit-
uary   **36**, 251
PARKER, Thomas M.
(Revd.) Frank Leslie Cross, 1900–
68. Obituary   **55**, 363
PARRY, Thomas
The Welsh Metrical Treatise, at-
tributed to Einion Offeiriad (JR)
47, 177
PARRY-WILLIAMS, T. H.
Welsh Poetic Diction (JR)
32, 243
PATON, H. J.
Can Reason be Practical? (P)
29, 65
Kant on Friendship (DH)   **42**, 45
PEARS, David
Predicting and Deciding (P)
50, 193
Naturalism in Book One of Hume's
Treatise of Human Nature (DH)
62, 249

PEERS, Sir C. R.
English Ornament in the Seventh and Eighth Centuries (AA)
12, 45
PELLIZZI, Camillo
Romanticism and Regionalism (I)
15, 135
PETRIE, Sir W. M. Flinders
Neglected British History   8, 251
PIGGOTT, Stuart
William Camden and the *Britannia* (AR)   37, 199
Vere Gordon Childe, 1892–1957. Obituary   44, 305
Sir Cyril Fox, 1882–1967. Obituary
53, 399
PIGOU, A. C.
John Maynard Keynes, 1883–1946. Obituary   32, 395
PIPER, David
The Development of the British Literary Portrait up to Samuel Johnson (AA)   54, 51
PLUMMER, Revd. Charles
On the Colophons and Marginalia of Irish Scribes   12, 11
POLLARD, A. F.
The Elizabethans and the Empire (R)   10, 139
POLLARD, Alfred W.
The Foundation of Shakespeare's Text (S)   10, 379
POLLOCK, Sir Frederick
Locke's Theory of the State 1, 237
Francis William Maitland, 1850–1906. Obituary   2, 455
Transliteration of Slavonic. Report of the Committee appointed by the Academy   8, 523
Sir Courtenay Peregrine Ilbert, 1841–1924. Obituary   11, 441
POOLE, Reginald L.
Léopold Delisle, 1826–1910 5, 203
Benedict IX and Gregory VI
8, 199
Imperial Influences on the Forms of Papal Documents   8, 237
Seals and Documents   9, 319

The Beginning of the Year in the Middle Ages   10, 113
The Early Correspondance of John of Salisbury   11, 27
POPE-HENNESSY, Sir John W.
The Italian Plaquette (AA) 50, 63
POPHAM, A. E.
Campbell Dodgson, 1867–1948. Obituary   36, 291
POPPER, Sir Karl R.
On the Sources of Knowledge and of Ignorance (P)   46, 39
PORTAL, Ethel M.
The Academ Roial of King James I
7, 189
POSTGATE, J. P.
Flaws in Classical Research 3, 161
On Ancient Greek Accentuation
11, 213
POWICKE, Sir F. M.
Thomas Frederick Tout, 1855–1929. Obituary   15, 491
Robert Grosseteste and the Nicomachaean Ethics   16, 85
Sir Henry Spelman and the 'Concilia' (R)   16, 345
(Revd.) Alexander James Carlyle, 1861–1943. Obituary (signed F. M. P.)   29, 313
The Compilation of the *Chronica Majora* of Matthew Paris 30, 147
James Tait, 1863–1944. Obituary
30, 379
Andrew George Little, 1863–1945. Obituary (signed F. M. P.)
31, 335
PRAZ, Mario
Machiavelli and the Elizabethans (I)   14, 49
PREVITÉ-ORTON, C. W.
Marsilius of Padua (I)   21, 137
PRICE, H. H.
Thinking and Representation (P)
32, 83
Harold Arthur Prichard, 1871–1947. Obituary   33, 331
PRICHARD, H. A.
Duty and Ignorance of Fact (P)
18, 67

PRINCE, F. T.
The Study of Form and the Renewal Of Poetry (W) **50**, 45
PRINGLE-PATTISON, A. Seth
Alexander Campbell Fraser, 1819–1914. Obituary **6**, 525
The Philosophy of History (P) **10**, 513
Richard Burdon Haldane, 1856–1928. Obituary **14**, 405
PRIOR, A. N.
Some Problems of Self-Reference in John Buridan (DH) **48**, 281
PUGH, Ralph B.
Some Reflections of a Medieval Criminologist (R) **59**, 83
PURSER, Louis C.
Robert Yelverton Tyrrell, 1844–1914. Obituary **7**, 533

Q

QUIGGIN, E. C.
Prolegomena to the Study of the Later Irish Bards, 1200–1500 **5**, 28
QUILLER-COUCH, Sir Arthur
Paternity in Shakespeare (S) **18**, 93
QUINTON, A. M.
Absolute Idealism (P) **57**, 303

R

RACKHAM, Revd. R. B.
The Nave of Westminster **4**, 33
RADCLIFFE, Philip
Edward Joseph Dent, 1876–1957. Obituary **62**, 411
RADFORD, C. A. Ralegh
Sir Charles Reed Peers, 1868–1952. Obituary **39**, 363
RADHAKRISHNAN, S.
Gautama the Buddha (MM) **24**, 143
RAINE, Kathleen
Waste Land, Holy Land (W) **62**, 379

RALEIGH, Sir Walter
Shakespeare and England (S) **8**, 403
RAMSAY, Sir William Mitchell
Excavation in Asia Minor **1**, 109
The Intermixture of Races in Asia Minor: Some of its Causes and Effects **7**, 359
RAMSEY, I. T.
(Revd.) Charles Earle Raven, 1885–1964. Obituary **51**, 467
RANDLE, H. N.
Frederick William Thomas, 1867–1956. Obituary **44**, 207
RAPHAEL, D. D.
Edgar Frederick Carritt, 1876–1964. Obituary **51**, 439
The Impartial Spectator (D.H) **58**, 335
RASHDALL, The Very Revd. Hastings
The Metaphysic of Mr F. H. Bradley **5**, 429
READE, W. H. V.
Dante's Vision of History (I) **25**, 187
REAY, Lord
President's Address at the First Annual General Meeting, 26 June 1903 **1**, 1
President's Address at the Second Annual General Meeting, 29 June 1904 **1**, 17
President's Address at the Third Annual General Meeting, 5 July 1905 **2**, 1
President's Address at the Fourth Annual General Meeting, 28 June 1906 **2**, 7
Sir Richard Jebb, a tribute **2**, 429
President's Address at the Fifth Annual General Meeting, 11 June 1907 **3**, 1
S. H. Butcher, 1850–1910. Obituary **4**, 390
Acting President's Address at the Ninth Annual General Meeting, 5 July 1911 **5**, 3
Sir A. C. Lyall, 1835–1911. Obituary **5**, 522

REID, Lord
The Law and the Reasonable Man (Mac) **54**, 189
REID, J. S.
Sir John Edwin Sandys, 1844–1922. Obituary **10**, 545
RENWICK, W. L.
'The Faerie Queene' (W) **33**, 149
RHŶS, Sir John
Studies in Early Irish History **1**, 21
Celtae and Galli **2**, 71
The Celtic Inscriptions of France and Italy **2**, 273
The Coligny Calendar **4**, 207
The Celtic Inscriptions of Gaul. Additions and Corrections **5**, 261
Gleanings in the Italian Field of Celtic Epigraphy **6**, 315
RICHARDS, G. C.
Alfred Chilton Pearson, 1861–1935. Obituary **21**, 449
RICHMOND, Rear Admiral Sir H. W.
National Policy and Naval Strength, XVIth to XXth Century (R) **10**, 339
RICHMOND, Sir I. A.
Robin George Collingwood, 1889–1943. Obituary **29**, 476
Roman Britain and Roman Military Antiquities (AR) **41**, 297
RICKS, Christopher
Tennyson's Methods of Composition (C) **52**, 209
RIDGEWAY, Sir William
The Date of the first shaping of the Cuchulainn Saga **2**, 135
Who were the Romans? **3**, 17
Minos the Destroyer rather than the Creator of the so-called 'Minoan' Culture of Cnossus **4**, 97
The Historical Background of the Later Irish Epic (the Cycle of Finn and Ossian) **4**, 343
RIDLEY, M. R.
On Reading Shakespeare (S) **26**, 197

RIGHTER, Anne
John Wilmot, Earl of Rochester (C) **53**, 47
RITCHIE, A. D.
George Berkeley's *SIRIS*: The Philosophy of the Great Chain of Being and the Alchemical Theory (P) **40**, 41
ROBBINS, Lord
Presidential Address, 10 July 1963 **49**, 43
Presidential Address, 8 July 1964 **50**, 37
Presidential Address, 7 July 1965 **51**, 39
Comments by the President at the AGM, 1966 **52**, 41
Of Academic Freedom (TOB) **52**, 45
Presidential Address, 12 July 1967 **53**, 39
The International Monetary Problem (K) **58**, 293
ROBERTS, C. H.
The Codex **40**, 169
Sir Harold Idris Bell, 1879–1967. Obituary **53**, 409
ROBERTS, S. C.
Samuel Johnson (MM) **30**, 51
ROBERTS, W. Rhys
Greek Civilisation as a Study for the People **7**, 505
ROBERTSON, Sir Charles Grant
John Henry Muirhead, 1855–1940. Obituary **26**, 381
Sir Charles Oman, 1860–1946. Obituary **32**, 299
ROBERTSON, J. G.
Milton's Fame on the Continent **3**, 319
Charles Harold Herford, 1853–1931. Obituary **17**, 401
ROBINSON, E. Austin G.
John Maynard Keynes: Economist, Author, Statesman (K) **57**, 197
ROBINSON, Sir Edward S. G.
The Date of the Roman Denarius and other Landmarks in Early Roman Coinage **18**, 211

ROBINSON, Sir Edward S. G. (*cont.*):
(Sir) George Francis Hill, 1867–
1948. Obituary   36, 241
John Walker, 1900–64. Obituary
52, 287
ROBINSON, J. Armitage
An Unrecognized Westminster
Chronicler 1381–1394   3, 61
ROBSON, W. W.
Byron as Poet (C)   43, 25
RODD, Sir Rennell
The Italian People (1)   9, 389
ROSE, H. J.
Wallace Martin Lindsay, 1858–
1937. Obituary   23, 487
Robert Ranulph Marett, 1866–
1943. Obituary   29, 357
ROSE, J. Holland
Was the Failure of the Spanish
Armada due to Storms? 22, 207
ROSS, Sir E. Denison
Marco Polo and his Book (I)
20, 181
ROSS, Sir W. David
Presidential Address, 14 July 1937
23, 21
Presidential Address, July 1938
24, 21
Presidential Address, 12 July 1939
25, 23
Presidential Address, 10 July 1940
26, 19
John Henry Muirhead, 1855–1940.
Obituary   26, 385
Alfred Edward Taylor, 1869–1945.
Obituary   31, 407
Clement Charles Julian Webb,
1865–1954. Obituary   41, 339
The Development of Aristotle's
Thought (DH)   43, 63
ROSTOVTZEFF, M.
Early Christian and Judaean Art in
Mesopotamia: Recent Discoveries
at Dura-Europos   19, 319
ROUTLEDGE, Mrs Scoresby
Easter Island Expedition   8, 133
ROWSE, A. L.
Sir Richard Grenville's Place in
English History (R)   43, 79

Richard Pares, 1902–58. Obituary
48, 345
RUBINSTEIN, Nicolai
Lorenzo de'Medici: The Formation
of His Statecraft (I)   63, 71
RUNCIMAN, Hon. Sir Steven
William Miller, 1864–1945. Obit-
uary   62, 513
RUSSELL, Bertrand (Earl)
John Stuart Mill (MM)   41, 43
RUSSELL, L. J.
The Concrete Background of Philo-
sophy (P)   37, 51
RUTHERFORD, Andrew
Some Aspects of Kipling's Verse (C)
51, 375
RYLANDS, George
Shakespeare's Poetic Energy (S)
37, 99
RYLE, Gilbert
A Puzzling Element in the Notion
of Thinking (P)   44, 129

S

SACKVILLE-WEST, Vita
Walter de la Mare and *The Traveller*
(W)   39, 23
SADLER, Sir Michael Ernest
The Ferment in Education on the
Continent and in America 1, 81
SAINTSBURY, George
The Historical Character of English
Lyric (W)   5, 475
Some Recent Studies in English
Prosody   9, 79
SALTER, Elizabeth
Medieval Poetry and the Figural
View of Reality (IG)   54, 73
SALTER, Lord
Lord Beveridge, 1879–1963. Obit-
uary   49, 417
SAMPSON, George
The Century of Divine Songs (W)
29, 37
SANDAY, Revd. W.
John Wordsworth (Bishop of Salis-
bury 1885–1911), 1843–1911.
Obituary   5, 530

SANDBACH, F. H.
Reginald Hackforth, 1887–1957.
Obituary **44**, 297
Donald Struan Robertson, 1885–
1961. Obituary **48**, 411
SANDERSON, Lord
Evelyn Earl of Cromer, GCB, OM,
Hon. Fellow of the Academy,
1841–1917. Obituary **8**, 552
SANDYS, Sir John Edwin
J. E. B. Mayor, 1825–1910. Obit-
uary **4**, 383
Roger Bacon **6**, 371
SANTAYANA, George
Philosophical Opinion in America
(P) **8**, 299
SAXL, F.
Costumes and Festivals of Milanese
Society under Spanish Rule
23, 401
SAYCE, Revd. A. H.
David George Hogarth, 1862–1927.
Obituary **13**, 379
SAYERS, R. S.
Thomas Southcliffe Ashton, 1889–
1968. Obituary **56**, 263
SAYLES, G. O.
Henry Gerald Richardson, 1884–
1974. Obituary **61**, 497
SCHLUMBERGER, Daniel
The Excavations at Surkh Kotal
and the Problem of Hellenism in
Bactria and India (RA) **47**, 77
SCHOLDERER, Victor
Printers and Readers in Italy in
the Fifteenth Century (I) **35**, 25
(Sir) Henry Thomas, 1878–1952.
Obituary **40**, 241
SCHRECKER, Paul
Leibniz: Ses idées sur l'Organisa-
tion des Relations Internationales
(MM) **23**, 193
SCHÜCKING, L. L.
The Baroque Character of the
Elizabethan Tragic Hero (S)
24, 85
SCOTT, W. R.
(The Ven.) William Cunningham,
1849–1919. Obituary **9**, 465

Adam Smith (MM) **10**, 435
Alfred Marshall, 1842–1924. Obit-
uary **11**, 446
Joseph Shield Nicholson, 1850–
1927. Obituary **13**, 346
Studies relating to Adam Smith
during the last Fifty Years
26, 249
SCRIPTURE, E. W.
The Study of English Speech by
new Methods of Phonetic In-
vestigation **10**, 271
SEGAL, J. B.
Mesopotamian Communities from
Julian to the Rise of Islam
41, 109
SELBIE, W. B.
Andrew Martin Fairbairn, 1838–
1912. Obituary **5**, 549
SELTMAN, Charles
Arthur Bernard Cook, 1868–1952.
Obituary **38**, 295
SETON-WATSON, R. W.
The Role of Bosnia in International
Politics (1875–1914) (R) **17**, 335
SHACKLE, G. L. S.
Time and Choice (K) **62**, 309
SHARROCK, Roger
The Figure in a Landscape: Words-
worth's Early Poetry (W) **58**, 313
SHAW, James Byam
Arthur Ewart Popham, 1889–1970.
Obituary **57**, 487
SHEARMAN, John
The Vatican Stanze: Functions and
Decoration (I) **57**, 369
SHEPHERD, Geoffrey
The Nature of Alliterative Poetry
in Late Medieval England (IG)
56, 57
SHIRRAS, G. Findlay
James Bonar, 1852–1941. Obituary
27, 359
SIMMONS, Jack
Sir Reginald Coupland, 1884–1952.
Obituary **45**, 287
SIMPSON, Percy
The Theme of Revenge in Eliza-
bethan Tragedy (S) **21**, 101

SINGER, Charles
Early English Magic and Medicine
9, 341
SISAM, Kenneth
Cynewulf and his Poetry (IG)
18, 303
Anglo-Saxon Royal Genealogies
39, 287
SISSON, C. J.
The Mythical Sorrows of Shake-
speare (S) 20, 45
Raymond Wilson Chambers, 1874–
1942. Obituary 30, 427
SKEAT, T. C.
The Use of Dictation in Ancient
Book-Production 42, 179
SKEAT, Revd. W. W.
The Problem of Spelling Reform
2, 247
John Peile, 1838–1910. Obituary
4, 379
SMITH, A. H.
Thomas Ashby, 1874–1931. Obit-
uary (signed A. H. S.) 17, 515
Horace William Brindley Joseph,
1867–1943. Obituary 31, 375
Place-Names and the Anglo-Saxon
Settlement (IG) 42, 67
SMITH, D. Mack
The Latifundia in Modern Sicilian
History 51, 85
SMITH, David Nichol
Warton's History of English Poetry
(W) 15, 73
SMITH, G. C. Moore
Thomas Randolph (W) 13, 79
SMITH, Sir G. Elliot
Primitive Man 7, 455
SMITH, Norman Kemp
Is Divine Existence Credible? (P)
17, 209
SMITH, Sidney
Sir Flinders Petrie, 1853–1942.
Obituary 28, 307
SORLEY, W. R.
The Interpretation of Evolution
4, 147
Josiah Royce, 1855–1916. Obituary
7, 585

Spinoza (MM) 8, 469
James Ward, 1843–1925. Obituary
12, 306
SOUTER, Alexander
The Commentary of Pelagius on the
Epistles of St. Paul: The Problem
of its Restoration 2, 409
The Character and History of
Pelagius' Commentary on the
Epistles of St. Paul 7, 261
James Smith Reid, 1846–1926. Obit-
uary 13, 335
SOUTHERN, R. W.
The Place of Henry I in English
History (R) 48, 127
Sir Maurice Powicke, 1879–1963.
Obituary 50, 275
SPARROW, John H. A.
Great Poetry (W) 46, 217
SPENCER, T. J. B.
The Tyranny of Shakespeare (S)
45, 153
SPURGEON, Caroline F. E.
Shakespeare's Iterative Imagery (S)
17, 147
STALLWORTHY, Jon
Wilfred Owen (C) 56, 241
STAROBINSKI, Jean
Rousseau (MM) 62, 95
STEBBING, L. Susan
Logical Positivism and Analysis (P)
19, 53
STEIN, Sir Aurel
Sir Thomas Walker Arnold, 1864–
1930. Obituary 16, 439
STEINBERG, S. H.
Stanley Morison, 1889–1967. Obit-
uary 53, 449
STENTON, Lady (Doris M.)
King John and the Courts of
Justice (R) 44, 103
(Sir) Frank Merry Stenton, 1880–
1967. Obituary 54, 315
STENTON, Sir Frank M.
The Danes in England (R) 13, 203
Sir Allen Mawer, 1879–1942. Obit-
uary 29, 433
STEWART, H. F.
Blaise Pascal (MM) 28, 197

T

STEWART, J. I. M.
Shakespeare's Lofty Scene (S)
57, 181

STONES, E. L. G.
Andrew Browning, 1889–1972.
Obituary 59, 427

STOUT, G. F.
Things and Sensations 2, 169
The Nature of Universals and
Propositions (P) 10, 157
Alexander Faulkner Shand, 1858–
1936. Obituary 22, 401

STRAWSON, P. F.
Freedom and Resentment (P)
48, 187

STUART, Lord Mackenzie
The 'Non-Contractual' Liability of
the European Economic Community (Mac) 61, 109

STUBBINGS, F. H.
Alan John Bayard Wace, 1879–
1957. Obituary 44, 263

SUMMERSON, Sir John
Inigo Jones (MM) 50, 169

SUMNER, B. H.
Tsardom and Imperialism in the
Far East and Middle East, 1880–
1914 (R) 27, 25

SUTHERLAND, C. H. V.
(Sir) Edward Stanley Gotch Robinson, 1887–1976. Obituary
63, 423

SUTHERLAND, James R.
Wordsworth and Pope (W)
30, 33
David Nichol Smith, 1875–1962.
Obituary 48, 449
John Everett Butt, 1906–65. Obit-
uary 52, 303

SUTHERLAND, Dame Lucy S.
The City of London and the Devonshire-Pitt Administration (R)
46, 147
Sir Lewis Namier, 1888–1960. Obituary 48, 371

SYME, Sir Ronald
Thucydides (MM) 48, 39

TAIT, James
The Study of Early Municipal
History in England 10, 201

TANNER, P. A. (Tony)
Problems and Roles of the American
Artist as Portrayed by the Ameri-
can Novelist (STP) 57, 159

TARN, W. W.
Seleucid-Parthian Studies 16, 105
Alexander the Great and the Unity
of Mankind (R) 19, 123

TAWNEY, R. H.
Harrington's Interpretation of his
Age (R) 27, 199
Beatrice Webb, 1858–1943. Obit-
uary 29, 285
J. L. Hammond, 1872–1949. Obit-
uary 46, 267

TAYLOR, A. E.
Plato's Biography of Socrates
8, 93
Francis Herbert Bradley, 1846–
1924. Obituary 11, 458
Francis Bacon (MM) 12, 273
John Burnet, 1863–1928. Obituary
14, 445
Plato and the Authorship of the
'Epinomis' 15, 235
William George de Burgh, 1866–
1943. Obituary 29, 371

TAYLOR, A. J.
Castle Building in Thirteenth Century Wales and Savoy (AR)
63, 265

TAYLOR, A. J. P.
Politics in the First World War (R)
45, 67

TAYLOR, Revd. Vincent
(Revd.) Wilbert Francis Howard,
1880–1952. Obituary 45, 277

TEDDER, H. R.
Lord Acton as a Book Collector.
Obituary 1, 285

TEMPERLEY, Harold
The Bulgarian and Other Atrocities,
1875–8, in the Light of Historical
Criticism 17, 105

TEMPLE, Sir Richard C.
William Crooke, 1848–1923. Obit-
uary   **10**, 576
TENNANT, Revd. F. R.
William Ritchie Sorley, 1855–1935.
Obituary   **21**, 393
John Wood Oman, 1860–1939.
Obituary   **25**, 333
THACKERAY, H. St. John
Sophocles and the Perfect Number
(A Neglected Nicety)   **16**, 15
THOMAS, Bertram
Four Strange Tongues from South
Arabia—The Hadara Group
                        23, 231
Arab Rule under the Al Bu Sa'id
Dynasty of Oman (R)   **24**, 27
THOMAS, D. Winton
Stanley Arthur Cook, 1873–1949.
Obituary   **36**, 261
THOMAS, F. W.
Arthur Anthony Macdonell, 1854–
1930. Obituary   **17**, 415
(Sir) George Abraham Grierson,
1851–1941. Obituary   **28**, 283
THOMAS, Sir Henry
Shakespeare in Spain (S)   **35**, 87
THOMAS, Keith
Age and Authority in Early Modern
England (R)   **62**, 205
THOMPSON, A. Hamilton
Diocesan Organisation in the
Middle Ages (R)   **29**, 153
THOMPSON, Sir E. Maunde
Alexander Stuart Murray. Obituary
                        1, 321
President's Address at the Sixth
Annual General Meeting, 25 June
1908   **3**, 7
President's Address at the Seventh
Annual General Meeting 1 July,
1909   **4**, 1
THOMPSON, Sir Herbert
Magical Texts from a Bilingual
Papyrus in the British Museum
                        17, 235
THOMPSON, R. Campbell
Harry Reginald Holland Hall, 1873–
1930. Obituary   **16**, 475

THOMPSON, Silvanus P.
Petrus Peregrinus de Maricourt and
his Epistola de Magnete   **2**, 377
The Rose of the Winds: The Origin
and Development of the Compass-
Card   **6**, 179
THOMSON, J. A. K.
Gilbert Murray, 1866–1957. Obit-
uary   **43**, 245
THOMSON, R. L.
The Study of Manx Gaelic (JR)
                        55, 177
THOMSON, S. Harrison
The 'Notule' of Grosseteste on the
Nicomachean Ethics   **19**, 195
THORNDIKE, Ashley
Shakespeare in America (S) **13**, 153
TILLOTSON, Geoffrey
The Manner of Proceeding in
Certain Eighteenth- and Early
Nineteenth-Century Poems (W)
                        34, 139
(Sir) Harold Herbert Williams,
1880–1964. Obituary   **51**, 455
TILLOTSON, Kathleen M.
Matthew Arnold and Carlyle (W)
                        42, 133
TILLYARD, E. M. W.
The English Epic Tradition (W)
                        22, 35
TOLKIEN, J. R. R.
Beowulf: The Monsters and the
Critics (IG)   **22**, 245
TOUT, T. F.
The Present State of Mediaeval
Studies in Great Britain   **6**, 151
Thomas Hodgkin, 1831–1913. Obit-
uary   **6**, 503
The Beginnings of a Modern Capital
—London and Westminster in
the Fourteenth Century (R)
                        10, 487
Sir Adolphus William Ward, 1837–
1924. Obituary   **11**, 427
Sir James Henry Ramsay, 1832–
1925. Obituary   **11**, 479
TOVEY, Sir Donald
The Main Stream of Music (AA)
                        24, 113

TOYNBEE, Jocelyn M. C.
The Ara Pacis Reconsidered and
Historical Art in Roman Italy (I)
39, 67
TOYNBEE, Paget
The Bearing of the 'Cursus' on the
Text of Dante's 'De Vulgari
Eloquentia' **10**, 359
TREHARNE, R. F.
The Personal Role of Simon de
Montfort in the Period of Baronial
Reform and Rebellion, 1258–65.
(R) **40**, 75
TREVELYAN, G. M.
Englishmen and Italians. Some
Aspects of their Relations Past
and Present (I) **9**, 91
Admiral Sir Herbert Richmond,
1871–1946. Obituary **32**, 325
TREVELYAN, Mrs G. M.
Wandering Englishmen in Italy (I)
16, 61
TRICKETT, Rachel
Browning's Lyricism (W) **57**, 65
TRYPANIS, C. A.
Eric Arthur Barber, 1888–1965.
Obituary **51**, 497
TURNER, E. G.
Derek Fortrose Allen, 1910–75.
Obituary **62**, 435
The Lost Beginning of Menander
Misoumenos **63**, 315
TYRELL, R. Y.
Sir Richard Claverhouse Jebb,
1841–1905. Obituary **2**, 445

U

ULLMANN, S.
Alfred Ewert, 1891–1969. Obituary
55, 377
URMSON, J. O.
The Objects of the Five Senses (P)
54, 117
URQUHART, W. S.
John Laird, 1887–1940. Obituary
32, 415

V

VAN HOONACKER A.
Note sur un Passage obscur de la
Lettre de Jedonja d'Eléphantine
à Bagohi, Gouverneur de Jéru-
salem **7**, 209
VAUGHAN, C.
The Influence of English Poetry
upon the Romantic Revival on
the Continent (W) **6**, 261
VENDRYES, J.
La Position Linguistique du Cel-
tique (JR) **23**, 333
VERHAEREN, Émile
An Aesthetic Interpretation of
Belgium's Past (AC) **8**, 81
VERRALL, A. W.
S. H. Butcher, 1850–1910. Obituary
4, 393
VILLARI, Commendatore Luigi
The Development of Political Ideas
in Italy in the Nineteenth Century
(I) **12**, 67
VINCENT, E. R.
Re-reading the Divine Comedy (I)
31, 223
VINCENT, John
Gladstone and Ireland (R)
63, 193
VINOGRADOFF, Sir Paul
Knight's Fees **3**, 15

W

WADE, Emlyn C. S.
Arnold Duncan McNair (Lord
McNair), 1885–1975. Obituary
62, 507
WADE, H. W. R.
Stanley Alexander de Smith, 1922–
74. Obituary **60**, 477
WAIN, John
Gerard Manley Hopkins: an Idiom
of Desperation (C) **45**, 173
WALEY, D. P.
Condotte and *Condottieri* in the
Thirteenth Century (I) **61**, 337

WALKER, Alice
Edward Capell and his Edition of
Shakespeare (S)   46, 131
WALKER, E. A.
Lord Milner and South Africa (R)
28, 155
WALKER, Hugh
The Revelation of England, through
her Poetry (W)   8, 181
WALKER, J.
John Allan, 1884–1955. Obituary
42, 303
WALPOLE, Sir Spencer
Mr Lecky. Obituary   1, 307
WALSH, W. H.
Kant's Moral Theology (DH)
49, 263
Herbert James Paton, 1887–1969.
Obituary   56, 293
WARD, Sir A. W.
Tercentenary of the Birth of John
Milton   3, 213
Presidential Address, 25 Oct 1911
5, 15
President's Address at the Tenth
Annual General Meeting, 1 July
1912   5, 7
Presidential Address, 30 Oct 1912
5, 23
Presidential Address, 1 July 1913
6, 1
Introductory and Supplementary
Remarks to the Presidential Ad-
dress of Lord Bryce at the Opening
Meeting of the International Con-
gress of Historical Studies, 3 April
1913   6, 113
Shakespeare and the Makers of
Virginia (S)   9, 141
WARD, James
Immanuel Kant (P)   10, 237
WARD-PERKINS, J. B.
The Italian Element in Late Roman
and Early Medieval Architecture
(I)   33, 163
The Art of the Severan Age in the
light of Tripolitanian Discoveries
37, 269

The Roman West and the Parthian
East   51, 175
Quarrying in Antiquity (MW)
57, 137
WARNOCK, G. J.
John Langshaw Austin, 1911–60.
Obituary   49, 345
The Primacy of Practical Reason
(DH)   52, 253
WATERHOUSE, Sir Ellis K.
The British Contribution to the
Neo-Classical Style in Painting
(AA)   40, 57
(Sir) Martin Davies, 1908–75. Obit-
uary   61, 561
WATSON, Sir Francis J. B.
Sir James Mann, 1897–1962. Obit-
uary   49, 407
WEBB, Clement C. J.
Our Knowledge of One Another (P)
16, 281
Reginald Lane Poole, 1857–1939.
Obituary   25, 311
WEBB, Geoffrey
Baroque Art (AA)   33, 131
WEBSTER, Sir Charles K.
Palmerston, Metternich, and the
European System 1830–1841 (R)
20, 125
Presidential Address, 11 July 1951
37, 15
Benedict Humphrey Sumner, 1893–
1951. Obituary   37, 359
Presidential Address, 6 June 1952
38, 13
Presidential Address, 8 July 1953
39, 15
Presidential Address, 7 July 1954
40, 15
WEISS, R.
The Greek Culture of South Italy in
the Later Middle Ages (I) 37, 23
WESTRUP, Sir Jack A.
The Nature of Recitative (AA)
42, 27
WHEARE, Sir Kenneth C.
Presidential Address, 10 July 1968
54, 45

Presidential Address, 9 July 1969
55, 45

Presidential Address, 8 July 1970
56, 51

Presidential Address, 7 July 1971
57, 59

Walter Bagehot (MM)   **60**, 173

George Derek Gordon Hall, 1924–75. Obituary   **62**, 427

WHEELER, Sir R. E. Mortimer
Wales and Archaeology (JR)
15, 319

WHINNEY, Margaret D.
Geoffrey Fairbank Webb, 1898–1970. Obituary   **57**, 453

WHITELOCK, Dorothy
The Old English Bede (IG) **48**, 57
Florence Elizabeth Harmer, 1890–1967. Obituary   **54**, 301

WICKENS, G. M.
Arthur John Arberry, 1905–69. Obituary   **58**, 355

WIGGINS, David
Truth, Invention, and the Meaning of Life (P)   **62**, 331

WILDE, Johannes
The Decoration of the Sistine Chapel (AA)   **44**, 61

WILKINSON, Elizabeth M.
Goethe's Conception of Form (MM)
37, 175

WILLCOCK, Gladys D.
Language and Poetry in Shakespeare's Early Plays (S)   **40**, 103

WILLEY, Basil
Coleridge on Imagination and Fancy (W)   **32**, 173
Helen Darbishire, 1881–1961. Obituary   **47**, 401
Eustace Mandeville Wetenhall Tillyard, 1889–1962. Obituary
49, 387
Henry Stanley Bennett, 1889–1972. Obituary   **58**, 551

WILLIAMS, B.
Sir George Otto Trevelyan, 1838–1928. Obituary   **16**, 383

WILLIAMS, Bernard
Imagination and the Self (P)
52, 105

WILLIAMS, Gordon
Eduard Fraenkel, 1888–1970. Obituary   **56**, 415

WILLIAMS, Ifor
The Poems of Llywarch Hên (JR)
18, 269

WILLIAMS, J. E. Caerwyn
The Court Poet in Medieval Ireland (JR)   **57**, 85

WILLIAMS, L. F. Rushbrook
The Cultural Significance of the Indian States   **16**, 203

WILSON, F. P.
Shakespeare and the Diction of Common Life (S)   **27**, 167
Sir Edmund Kerchever Chambers, 1866–1954. Obituary **42**, 277
Sir Walter Wilson Greg, 1875–1959. Obituary   **45**, 307

WILSON, J. Cook
David Binning Monro, Obituary
2, 449

WILSON, J. Dover
The Elizabethan Shakespeare (S)
15, 101
George Charles Moore Smith, 1858–1940. Obituary **30**, 361
Alfred William Pollard, 1859–1954. Obituary   **31**, 257
Sir Edmund Kerchever Chambers, 1866–1954. Obituary **42**, 267

WILSON, Thomas
The Political Economy of Inflation (K)   **61**, 291

WIND, Edgar
Michelangelo's Prophets and Sibyls (AA)   **51**, 47

WINFIELD, Sir P. H.
Sir William Searle Holdsworth, 1871–1944. Obituary (signed P. H. W.)   **30**, 414

WINNINGTON-INGRAM, R. P.
Amy Marjorie Dale, 1902–67. Obituary   **53**, 423

WINTER, C.
The British School of Miniature Portrait Painters (AA) **34**, 119

WISDOM, John
The Metamorphosis of Metaphysics (P) **47**, 37

WOLLHEIM, Richard A.
The Good Self and the Bad Self (DH) **61**, 373

WOODFORDE, Revd. Christopher
English Stained Glass and Glass-Painters in the Fourteenth Century (AA) **25**, 29

WOODWARD, Sir E. Llewellyn
Some Considerations on the Present State of Historical Studies (R) **36**, 95

WORDSWORTH, Jonathan
William Wordsworth 1770–1969 (C) **55**, 211

WORMALD, Francis
The Survival of Anglo-Saxon Illumination after the Norman Conquest (AA) **30**, 127
Paintings in Westminster Abbey and Contemporary Paintings (AA) **35**, 161

WRENN, C. L.
The Poetry of Cædmon (IG) **32**, 277

WRIGHT, C. E.
Humfrey Wanley: Saxonist and Library-Keeper (IG) **46**, 99

WRIGHT, Lord
Lord Atkin of Aberdovey, 1867–1944. Obituary **32**, 307

WYLLIE, J. M.
Sir William Craigie, 1867–1957. Obituary **47**, 273

WYNN, The Rt. Revd. Harold Edward, Bishop of Ely
(Revd.) James Franklin Bethune-Baker, 1861–1951. Obituary **39**, 355

Y

YOUNG, G. M.
The Age of Tennyson (W) **25**, 125
Burke (MM) **29**, 19
Shakespeare and the Termers (S) **33**, 81

Z

ZARNECKI, George
1066 and Architectural Sculpture (AA) **52**, 87

ZEPOS, Pan. J.
Jeremy Bentham and the Greek Independence (Ex.A) **62**, 293

ZHIRMUNSKY, Victor
The Epic of 'Altramysh' and the Return of Odysseus **52**, 267

ZUNTZ, Günther
The Interpretation of a Menander Fragment **42**, 209
On the Dionysiac Fresco in the Villa dei Misteri at Pompeii **49**, 177

INDEX OF MEMOIRS

A

ABERCROMBIE, Lascelles, 1881–1938
By O. Elton   **25**, 394
ACTON, Lord
By Viscount Bryce   **1**, 277
Lord Acton as a Cambridge Professor. By W. A. J. Archbold
1, 282
Lord Acton as a Book Collector. By H. R. Tedder   **1**, 285
ADCOCK, Sir Frank Ezra, 1886–1968
By N. G. L. Hammond   **54**, 425
ALLAN, John, 1884–1955
By J. Walker   **42**, 303
ALLEN, Sir Carleton Kemp, 1887–1966
By A. L. Goodhart   **53**, 391
ALLEN, Derek Fortrose, 1910–75
By E. G. Turner   **62**, 435
ALLEN, Percy Stafford, 1869–1933
By H. W. Garrod   **19**, 381
ARBERRY, Arthur John, 1905–69
By G. M. Wickens   **58**, 355
ARMSTRONG, Edward, 1846–1928
By W. H. Hutton   **14**, 395
ARNOLD, Sir Thomas Walker, 1864–1930
By Sir A. Stein   **16**, 439
ASHBY, Thomas, 1874–1931
By A. H. Smith (signed A. H. S.)
17, 515
ASHTON, Thomas Southcliffe, 1889–1968
By R. S. Sayers   **56**, 263
ATKIN OF ABERDOVEY, James Richard, Lord, 1867–1944
By Lord Wright   **32**, 307
AUSTIN, John Langshaw, 1911–60
By G. J. Warnock   **49**, 345

B

BAILEY, Cyril, 1871–1958
By W. Oakeshott   **46**, 295
BALFOUR, Arthur James (Earl of Balfour), 1848–1930
By Sir F. G. Kenyon   **16**, 410
BARBER, Eric Arthur, 1888–1965
By C. A. Trypanis   **51**, 497
BARING, Evelyn
see Cromer, Earl of
BARKER, Sir Ernest, 1874–1960
By G. E. G. Catlin   **46**, 341
BARNETT, Lionel David, 1871–1960
By A. L. Bashan   **46**, 333
BASTABLE, Charles Francis, 1855–1945
By G. A. Duncan   **31**, 241
BAYNES, Norman Hepburn, 1877–1961
By J. M. Hussey   **49**, 365
BEAZLEY, Sir John Davidson, 1885–1970
By B. Ashmole   **56**, 443
BELL, Sir Harold Idris, 1879–1967
By C. H. Roberts   **53**, 409
BENNETT, Henry Stanley, 1889–1972
By B. Willey   **58**, 551
BETHUNE-BAKER, Revd. James Franklin, 1861–1951
By the Rt. Revd. H. E. Wynn, Bishop of Ely   **39**, 355
BEVAN, Edwyn Robert, 1870–1943
By G. Murray (signed G. M.)
29, 411
BEVERIDGE, William, Lord, 1879–1963
By Lord Salter   **49**, 417
BLACKMAN, Aylward Manley, 1883–1956
By W. B. Emery   **44**, 225
BONAR, James, 1852–1941
By G. F. Shirras   **27**, 359

BOSANQUET, Bernard, 1848–1923
By A. C. Bradley and Viscount
Haldane **10**, 563
BOWRA, Sir C. Maurice, 1898–1971
By P. H. J. Lloyd-Jones **58**, 393
BRADLEY, Andrew Cecil, 1851–1935
By J. W. Mackail **21**, 385
BRADLEY, Francis Herbert, 1846–1924
By A. E. Taylor **11**, 458
BRIGHTMAN, Revd. Frank Edward,
1856–1932
By H. N. Bate **19**, 345
BROGAN, Sir Denis William, 1900–
74
By H. G. Nicholas **62**, 399
BROOKE, Revd. Alan England, 1863–
1939
By Revd. J. F. Bethune-Baker
26, 439
BROOKE, Zachary Nugent, 1883–1946
By Helen M. Cam **32**, 381
BROWN, Gerard Baldwin, 1849–1932
By Sir G. Macdonald **21**, 375
BROWN, Peter Hume, 1849–1918
By Sir G. Macdonald **8**, 591
BROWNING, Andrew, 1889–1972
By E. L. G. Stones **59**, 427
BRYCE, James, Viscount Bryce of
Dechmont, 1838–1922
By H. A. L. Fisher **12**, 297
BUCKLAND, William Warwick, 1859–
1946
By Sir A. D. McNair (Lord
McNair), and P. W. Duff
33, 283
BUCKLER, William Hepburn, 1867–
1952
By Sir W. M. Calder **40**, 275
BURKITT, Francis Crawford, 1864–
1935
By Revd. J. F. Bethune-Baker
22, 445
BURNET, John, 1863–1928
By W. L. Lorimer and A. E.
Taylor **14**, 445
BURT, Sir Cyril Lodowic, 1883–1971
By L. S. Hearnshaw **58**, 475
BURY, John Bagnell, 1861–1927
By N. H. Baynes **13**, 368

BUTCHER, S. Henry, 1850–1910
By Lord Reay **4**, 390
By A. W. Verrall **4**, 393
BUTT, John Everett, 1906–65
By J. R. Sutherland **52**, 303
BYWATER, Ingram, 1840–1914
By W. W. Jackson **7**, 521

C

CAIRD, Edward, 1835–1908
By B. Bosanquet **3**, 379
CALDER, Sir William Moir, 1881–1960
By J. M. R. Cormack **47**, 345
CAM, Helen Maude, 1885–1968
By C. R. Cheney **55**, 293
CARLYLE, Revd. Alexander James,
1861–1943
By Sir F. M. Powicke (signed F. M.
P.) **29**, 313
CARR, Sir Cecil Thomas, 1878–1966
By H. A. Hollond **52**, 311
CARR-SAUNDERS, Sir Alexander
Morris, 1886–1966
By Sir H. Phelps Brown **53**, 379
CARRITT, Edgar Frederick, 1876–1964
By D. D. Raphael **51**, 439
ČERNÝ, Jaroslav, 1898–1970
By I. E. S. Edwards **58**, 367
CHADWICK, Hector Munro, 1870–1947
By J. M. de Navarro **33**, 307
CHADWICK, Nora Kershaw, 1891–1972
By K. H. Jackson **58**, 537
CHALMERS, Lord, 1858–1938
By P. E. Matheson **25**, 321
CHAMBERS, Sir Edmund Kerchever,
1866–1954
By F. P. Wilson and J. Dover
Wilson **42**, 267
CHAMBERS, Raymond Wilson, 1874–
1942
By C. J. Sisson **30**, 427
CHAPMAN, Robert William, 1881–1960
By Mary Lascelles **47**, 361
CHARLES, The Ven. Archdeacon
Robert Henry, 1855–1931
By F. C. Burkitt **17**, 437

CHARLESWORTH, Revd. Martin Percival, 1895–1950
By Sir F. E. Adcock   **36**, 277
CHEYNE, Revd. Thomas Kelly, 1841–1915
By the Ven. R. H. Charles **7**, 545
CHILDE, Vere Gordon, 1892–1957
By S. Piggot   **44**, 305
CLAPHAM, Sir Alfred William, 1883–1950
By W. H. Godfrey   **39**, 351
CLAPHAM, Sir John Harold, 1873–1946
By Sir G. N. Clark   **32**, 339
CLARK, Albert Curtis, 1859–1937
By C. Bailey   **23**, 513
COLLINGWOOD, Robin George, 1889–1943
By R. B. McCallum, J. M. Knox, and Sir I. A. Richmond **29**, 463
CONWAY, Robert Seymour, 1864–1933
By C. Bailey   **22**, 434
CONYBEARE, Frederick Cornwallis, 1856–1924
By A. C. Clark and J. R. Harris   **11**, 469
COOK, Arthur Bernard, 1868–1952
By C. Seltman   **38**, 295
COOK, Stanley Arthur, 1873–1949
By D. W. Thomas   **36**, 261
CORNFORD, Francis Macdonald, 1874–1943
By G. Murray   **29**, 421
COULTON, George Gordon, 1858–1947
By H. S. Bennett   **33**, 267
COUPLAND, Sir Reginald, 1884–1952
By J. Simmons   **45**, 287
COURTHOPE, William John, 1842–1917
By J. W. Mackail   **8**, 581
COWELL, Edward Byles
By T. W. R. Davids   **1**, 302
COWLEY, Sir Arthur Ernest, 1861–1931
By T. W. Allen   **19**, 351
CRAIGIE, Sir William Alexander, 1867–1957
By J. M. Wyllie   **47**, 273

CRAWFORD, Osbert Guy Stanhope, 1886–1957
By Sir G. N. Clark   **44**, 281
CREED, Revd. John Martin, 1889–1940
By Revd. J. F. Bethune-Baker   **26**, 517
CRESWELL, Sir Keppel Archibald Cameron, 1879–1974
By R. W. Hamilton   **60**, 459
CROCE, Benedetto, 1866–1952
By E. F. Carritt   **38**, 345
CROMER, Evelyn Earl of, 1841–1917
By Lord Sanderson   **8**, 552
CROOKE, William, 1848–1923
By Sir R. C. Temple   **10**, 576
CROSS, Revd. Frank Leslie, 1900–68
By T. M. Parker   **55**, 363
CRUM, Walter Ewing, 1865–1944
By B. Gunn and Sir H. I. Bell   **34**, 281
CUNNINGHAM, The Ven. Archdeacon William, 1849–1919
By W. R. Scott   **9**, 465
CURZON, George Nathaniel, Marquis Curzon of Kedleston, 1865–1925
By D. G. Hogarth   **11**, 502

D

DALE, Amy Marjorie, 1902–67 (Mrs Madge Webster)
By R. P. Winnington-Ingram   **53**, 423
DALTON, Ormonde Maddock, 1866–1945
By Sir G. F. Hill   **31**, 357
DARBISHIRE, Helen, 1881–1961
By B. Willey   **47**, 401
D'ARCY, The Most Revd. Charles Frederick, 1859–1938
By A. A. Luce   **24**, 361
DAVEY, Lord, 1833–1907
By Sir C. P. Ilbert   **3**, 371
DAVIDS, Thomas William Rhys, 1843–1922
By Lord Chalmers   **10**, 540

DAVIDSON, Andrew Bruce
By Revd. S. R. Driver   **1**, 289
DAVIES, Sir Martin, 1908–75
By Sir E. Waterhouse   **61**, 561
DAVIS, Herbert John, 1893–1967
By Dame Helen Gardner   **54**, 289
DAWKINS, Richard MacGillivray, 1871–1955
By R. J. H. Jenkins   **41**, 373
DAWSON, Christopher, 1889–1970
By Revd. M. D. Knowles   **57**, 439
DE BURGH, William George, 1866–1943
By A. E. Taylor   **29**, 371
DENNISTON, John Dewar, 1887–1949
By Sir C. M. Bowra   **35**, 219
DENT, Edward Joseph, 1876–1957
By P. Radcliffe   **62**, 411
DE SELINCOURT, Ernest, 1870–1943
By Helen Darbishire   **29**, 393
DE SMITH, Stanley Alexander, 1922–74
By H. W. R. Wade   **60**, 477
DILLON, Harold Arthur, Viscount, 1844–1932
By C. ffoulkes   **18**, 335
DOBB, Maurice Herbert, 1900–76
By R. M. Meek   **63**, 333
DODD, Revd. Charles Harold, 1884–1973
By Revd. G. B. Caird   **60**, 497
DODGSON, Campbell, 1867–1948
By A. E. Popham   **36**, 291
DRIVER, Sir Godfrey Rolles, 1892–1975
By J. A. Emerton   **63**, 345
DRIVER, Revd. Samuel Rolles, 1846–1914
By Sir A. E. Cowley   **7**, 540
DUNDAS, *see* Zetland, Marquess of

E

ELLIS, Robinson, 1834–1913
By A. C. Clark   **6**, 517
ELTON, Oliver, 1861–1945
By L. C. Martin   **31**, 317
EMERY, Walter Bryan, 1903–71
By A. Klasens   **58**, 379

ENTWISTLE, William James, 1895–1952
By A. Ewert   **38**, 333
EVANS, Sir Arthur John, 1851–1941
By Sir J. L. Myres   **27**, 323
EWERT, Alfred, 1891–1969
By S. Ullmann   **55**, 377
EWING, Alfred Cyril, 1899–1973
By G. R. Grice   **59**, 499

F

FAIRBAIRN, Revd. Andrew Martin, 1838–1912
By W. B. Selbie   **5**, 549
FARNELL, Lewis Richard, 1856–1934
By R. R. Marett   **20**, 285
FARRER, Revd. Austin Marsden, 1904–68
By Revd. E. L. Mascall   **54**, 435
FIELD, Guy Cromwell, 1887–1955
By D. J. Allan   **42**, 311
FIFOOT, Cecil Herbert Stuart, 1899–1975
By G. C. Cheshire   **61**, 429
FIRTH, Sir Charles Harding, 1857–1936
By G. Davies   **22**, 380
FISHER, Herbert Albert Laurens, 1865–1940
By G. Murray (signed G. M.)   **26**, 455
FLOWER, Sir Cyril Thomas, 1879–1961
By Sir D. L. Evans   **48**, 387
FLOWER, Robin Ernest William, 1881–1946
By Sir H. I. Bell   **32**, 353
FORDE, Cyril Daryll, 1902–73
By M. Fortes   **62**, 459
FOTHERINGHAM, John Knight, 1874–1936
By Sir J. L. Myres   **23**, 551
FOX, Sir Cyril, 1882–1967
By S. Piggot   **53**, 399
FOXWELL, Herbert Somerton, 1849–1936
By Lord Keynes (signed J. M. K.)   **23**, 470

FRAENKEL, Eduard, 1888–1970
  By G. Williams   56, 415
FRANKFORT, Henri, 1897–1954
  By V. G. Childe   41, 367
FRASER, Alexander Campbell, 1819–
  1914
  By A. S. Pringle-Pattison   6, 525
FRAZER, Sir James George, 1854–1941
  By R. R. Marett   26, 377
FURNIVALL, Frederick James, 1825–
  1910
  By W. P. Ker   4, 375

G

GADD, Cyril John, 1893–1969
  By Sir M. Mallowan   56, 363
GARDINER, Sir Alan Henderson, 1879–
  1963
  By J. Černý   50, 263
GARDINER, Samuel Rawson
  By Sir C. H. Firth   1, 295
GARDNER, Edmund Garratt, 1869–
  1935
  By C. Foligno   21, 464
GARDNER, Percy, 1846–1937
  By Sir G. F. Hill   23, 459
GARROD, Dorothy Annie Elizabeth,
  1892–1968
  By Gertrude Caton-Thompson
                                55, 339
GARROD, Heathcote William, 1878–
  1960
  By J. Jones   48, 357
GASELEE, Sir Stephen, 1882–1943
  By A. S. F. Gow   29, 441
GIBB, Sir Hamilton Alexander Ros-
  keen, 1895–1971
  By A. Hourani   58, 493
GILES, Peter, 1860–1935
  By R. M. Dawkins   21, 406
GLANVILLE, Stephen Ranulph King-
  don, 1900–56
  By I. E. S. Edwards   44, 231
GLUCKMAN, H. Max, 1911–75
  By Sir R. W. Firth   61, 479
GOLLANCZ, Sir Israel, 1863–1930
  By Sir F. G. Kenyon   16, 424

GOMME, Arnold Wycombe, 1886–1959
  By H. D. F. Kitto   45, 335
GOOCH, George Peabody, 1873–1968
  By Sir H. Butterfield   55, 311
GOSCHEN, George Joachim, First Vis-
  count, 1831–1907
  By Viscount Milner   3, 359
GREG, Sir Walter Wilson, 1875–1959
  By F. P. Wilson   45, 307
GRENFELL, Bernard Pyne, 1869–1926
  By A. S. Hunt   12, 357
GRIERSON, Sir George Abraham,
  1851–1941
  By F. W. Thomas and Sir R. L.
  Turner   28, 283
GRIERSON, Sir Herbert John Clifford,
  1866–1960
  By D. Daiches   46, 319
GRIFFITH, Francis Llewellyn, 1862–
  1934
  By W. E. Crum   20, 309
GUNN, Battiscombe George, 1883–
  1950
  By W. R. Dawson   36, 259
GUTHRIE, Malcolm, 1903–72
  By Hazel Carter   59, 473

H

HACKFORTH, Reginald, 1887–1957
  By F. H. Sandbach   44, 297
HALDANE, Richard Burdon, Viscount
  Haldane, 1856–1928
  By A. S. Pringle-Pattison   14, 405
HALL, George Derek Gordon, 1924–75
  By Sir K. C. Wheare   62, 427
HALL, Harry Reginald Holland,
  1873–1930
  By R. Campbell Thompson
                                16, 475
HAMMOND, John Lawrence Le Breton,
  1872–1949
  By R. H. Tawney   46, 267
HARMER, Florence Elizabeth, 1890–
  1967
  By Dorothy Whitelock   54, 301
HAVERFIELD, Francis John, 1860–1919
  By Sir G. Macdonald   9, 475

HAWTREY, Sir Ralph George, 1879–1975
By R. D. C. Black   **63**, 363
HAZELTINE, Harold Dexter, 1871–1960
By H. A. Hollond   **47**, 311
HEATH, Sir Thomas Little, 1861–1940
By M. F. Headlam   **26**, 425
HERFORD, Charles Harold, 1853–1931
By J. G. Robertson   **17**, 401
HICKS, George Dawes, 1862–1941
By W. G. de Burgh   **27**, 405
HIGGINS, Alexander Pearce, 1865–1935
By Sir A. D. McNair (Lord McNair)   **22**, 485
HILL, Sir George Francis, 1867–1948
By Sir E. S. G. Robinson   **36**, 241
HOBHOUSE, Leonard Trelawney, 1864–1929
By Sir E. Barker   **15**, 536
HODGKIN, Thomas, 1831–1913
By T. F. Tout   **6**, 503
HODGSON, Shadworth Holloway, 1832–1913
By G. D. Hicks   **6**, 508
HOGARTH, David George, 1862–1927
By Revd. A. H. Sayce   **13**, 379
HOLDSWORTH, Sir William Searle, 1871–1944
By R. W. Lee (signed R. W. L.) and Sir P. H. Winfield (signed P. H. W.)   **30**, 411
HOLLAND, Sir Thomas Erskine, 1835–1926
By Sir W. S. Holdsworth   **12**, 317
HOLMES, Thomas Rice Edward, 1855–1933
Unsigned   **22**, 358
HOWARD, Revd. Wilbert Francis, 1880–1952
By Revd. V. Taylor   **45**, 277
HUNT, ARTHUR Surridge, 1871–1934
By Sir H. I. Bell   **20**, 323
HUTCHINSON, (Revd. Canon) Francis Ernest, 1871–1947
By K. M. Lea   **45**, 269

I

ILBERT, Sir Courtenay Peregrine, 1841–1924
By Sir F. Pollock   **11**, 441
INGE, The Very Revd. William Ralph, 1860–1954
By the Very Revd. W. R. Matthews   **40**, 263

J

JACOB, Ernest Fraser, 1894–1971
By W. A. Pantin   **58**, 447
JAMES, Montague Rhodes, 1862–1936
By Sir S. Gaselee   **22**, 418
JEBB, Sir Richard Claverhouse, 1841–1905
By Lord Reay   **2**, 443
By R. Y. Tyrrell   **2**, 445
JENKS, Edward, 1861–1939
By R. W. Lee   **26**, 399
JOACHIM, Harold Henry, 1868–1938
By H. W. B. Joseph   **24**, 396
JOHNSON, Charles, 1870–1961
By H. C. Johnson   **51**, 403
JOHNSON, William Ernest, 1858–1931
By C. D. Broad   **17**, 491
JONES, Arnold Hugh Martin, 1904–70
By J. A. Crook   **57**, 425
JONES, Sir Henry, 1852–1922
By J. H. Muirhead   **10**, 552
JONES, Sir Henry Stuart, 1867–1939
By Sir J. L. Myres (signed J. L. M.)   **26**, 467
JONES, William Henry Samuel, 1876–1963
By Sir F. E. Adcock   **49**, 413
JOSEPH, Horace William Brindley, 1867–1943
By A. H. Smith   **31**, 375

K

KAHLE, Paul Ernst, 1875–1965
By the Very Revd. M. Black   **51**, 485

KENNEDY, Lord Justice William Rann, 1846–1915
By Sir T. E. Holland **7**, 552
KENNY, Courtenay Stanhope, 1847–1930
By H. D. Hazeltine **18**, 345
KENYON, Sir Frederick George, 1863–1952
By Sir H. I. Bell **38**, 269
KER, William Paton, 1855–1923
By R. W. Chambers **11**, 413
KERSHAW, Nora,
see Chadwick, Nora Kershaw
KETTON-CREMER, Robert Wyndham, 1906–69
By Mary M. Lascelles **56**, 403
KEYNES, John Maynard (Lord Keynes) 1883–1946
By A. C. Pigou **32**, 395
KINGSFORD, Charles Lethbridge, 1862–1926
By A. G. Little **12**, 348
KNOWLES, Revd. M. David, 1896–1974
By C. N. L. Brooke **61**, 439
KNOX, Revd. Wilfred Lawrence, 1886–1950
By Revd. C. H. Dodd **47**, 263

LEE, Robert Warden, 1868–1958
By H. G. Hanbury **44**, 313
LEE, Sir Sidney, 1859–1926
By Sir C. H. Firth **15**, 445
LEISHMAN, James Blair, 1902–63
By J. E. Butt **49**, 459
LEWIS, Clive Staples, 1898–1963
By Dame Helen Gardner **51**, 417
LIEBERMANN, Felix, 1851–1925
By H. D. Hazeltine **24**, 319
LIGHTFOOT, Revd. Robert Henry, 1883–1953
By the Very Revd. Canon R. L. P. Milburn **40**, 253
LINDSAY, Wallace Martin, 1858–1937
By H. J. Rose **23**, 487
LITTLE, Andrew George, 1863–1945
By Sir F. M. Powicke (signed F. M. P.) **31**, 335
LLOYD, Sir John Edward, 1861–1947
By J. G. Edwards **41**, 319
LORIMER, William Laughton, 1885–1967
By K. J. Dover **53**, 437
LYALL, Sir Alfred Comyn, 1835–1911
By Lord Reay **5**, 522
By Sir C. P. Ilbert **5**, 525
LYALL, Sir Charles James, 1845–1920
By R. A. Nicholson **9**, 492

L

LAIRD, John, 1887–1940
By W. S. Urquhart **32**, 415
LANG, Andrew, 1844–1912
By P. Hume Brown **5**, 552
LANGDON, Stephen Herbert, 1876–1937
By C. J. Gadd **23**, 565
LAUTERPACHT, Sir Hersch, 1897–1960
By Lord McNair **47**, 371
LEA, Henry Charles, 1825–1909
By E. P. Cheyney **5**, 517
LEAKEY, Louis Seymour Bazett, 1903–72
By J. Desmond Clark **59**, 447
LECKY, William Edward Hartpole
By Sir S. Walpole **1**, 307

M

MACDONALD, Sir George, 1862–1940
By A. O. Curle **27**, 433
MACDONELL, Arthur Anthony, 1854–1930
By F. W. Thomas **17**, 415
McFARLANE, K. B., 1903–66
By K. J. Leyser **62**, 485
(*see* erratum slip in vol. 63)
MACKAIL, John William, OM, 1859–1945
By C. Bailey **31**, 245
MACKAY, Donald James
see Reay, Lord
MACKENZIE, John Stuart, 1860–1935
By J. H. Muirhead **21**, 433

McKerrow, Ronald Brunlees, 1872–
1940
By Sir W. W. Greg   26, 489
McLean, Norman, 1865–1947
By H. St. J. Hart   63, 399
McNair, Andrew Duncan (Lord
McNair), 1885–1975
By E. C. S. Wade   62, 507
McTaggart, John McTaggart Ellis,
1866–1925
By C. D. Broad   13, 307
Maitland, Frederick William, 1850–
1906
By Sir F. Pollock   2, 455
Mann, Sir James G., 1897–1962
By Sir F. J. B. Watson   49, 407
Manson, Revd. Thomas Walter,
1893–1958
By the Very Revd. M. Black
44, 325
Marett, Robert Ranulph, 1866–1943
By H. J. Rose   29, 357
Margoliouth, David Samuel, 1858–
1940
By G. Murray   26, 389
Marshall, Alfred, 1842–1924
By W. R. Scott   11, 446
Mattingly, Harold, 1884–1964
By R. A. G. Carson   50, 331
Mawer, Sir Allen, 1879–1942
By Sir F. M. Stenton   29, 433
Maxwell-Lyte, Sir Henry Churchill,
1848–1940
By C. Johnson   26, 361
Mayor, Revd. John Eyton Bicker-
steth, 1825–1910
By Sir J. E. Sandys   4, 383
Miller, William, 1864–1945
By the Hon. Sir S. Runciman
62, 513
Monro, David Binning, 1836–1905
By J. Cook Wilson   2, 449
Moore, Revd. Canon Edward, 1835–
1916
By E. Armstrong   7, 575
Moore, George Edward, 1873–1958
By R. B. Braithwaite   47, 293
Morfill, William Richard, 1834–1909
By Sir J. A. H. Murray   4, 368

Morison, Stanley Arthur, 1889–1967
By S. H. Steinberg   53, 449
Muirhead, John Henry, 1855–1940
By Sir C. Grant Robertson and Sir
W. D. Ross   26, 381
Murray, Alexander Stuart
By Sir E. M. Thompson   1, 321
Murray, Gilbert, 1866–1957
By J. A. K. Thomson   43, 245
Murray, Sir James A. H., 1837–1915
By H. Bradley   8, 545
Myres, Sir John Linton, 1869–1954
By T. J. Dunbabin   41, 349

N

Namier, Sir Lewis Bernstein, 1888–
1960
By Dame Lucy S. Sutherland
48, 371
Neale, Sir John Ernest, 1890–1975
By J. Hurstfield   63, 403
Nicholson, Joseph Shield, 1850–1927
By W. R. Scott   13, 346
Nicholson, Reynold Alleyne, 1868–
1945
By R. Levy   31, 399

O

Oman, Sir Charles William Chad-
wick, 1860–1946
By Sir C. Grant Robertson   32, 299
Oman, Revd. John Wood, 1860–1939
By Revd. F. R. Tennant   25, 333
Orr, John, 1885–1966
By A. Ewert   52, 323

P

Pantin, William Abel, 1902–73
By Revd. M. D. Knowles   60, 447
Pares, Richard, 1902–58
By A. L. Rowse   48, 345
Parsons, Doris Mary
see Stenton, Doris Mary

PATON, Herbert James, 1887–1969
By W. H. Walsh   56, 293
PEARSON, Alfred Chilton, 1861–1935
By G. C. Richards   21, 449
PEERS, Sir Charles Reed, 1868–1952
By C. A. R. Radford   39, 363
PEILE, John, 1838–1910
By Revd. W. W. Skeat   4, 379
PELHAM, Henry Francis, 1846–1907
By F. J. Haverfield   3, 365
PETRIE, Sir William Matthew Flin-
ders, 1853–1942
By S. Smith   28, 307
PICKARD-CAMBRIDGE, Sir Arthur Wal-
lace, 1873–1952
By C. Bailey   38, 303
PLAMENATZ, John Petrov, 1912–75
By G. Marshall   62, 419
PLUCKNETT, Theodore Frank Thomas,
1897–1965
By S. F. C. Milsom   51, 505
PLUMMER, Revd. Charles, 1851–1927
By P. S. Allen   15, 463
POLLARD, Albert Frederick, 1869–
1948
By V. H. Galbraith   35, 257
POLLARD, Alfred William, 1859–1944
By J. Dover Wilson   31, 257
POLLOCK, Sir Frederick, Bart, 1845–
1937
By H. D. Hazeltine   35, 233
POOLE, Austin Lane, 1889–1963
By V. H. Galbraith   49, 431
POOLE, REGINALD LANE, 1857–1939
By C. C. J. Webb   25, 311
POPHAM, Arthur Ewart, 1889–1970
By J. Byam Shaw   57, 487
POSTGATE, John Percival, 1853–1926
By S. G. Owen   12, 337
POWICKE, Sir Frederick Maurice,
1879–1963
By R. W. Southern   50, 275
PRESTAGE, Edgar, 1869–1951
By C. R. Boxer   44, 199
PREVITÉ-ORTON, C. W., 1877–1947
By Revd. M. D. Knowles   33, 351
PRICHARD, Harold Arthur, 1871–1947
By H. H. Price   33, 331

PRINGLE-PATTISON,   Andrew   Seth,
1856–1931
By J. B. Capper and J. B. Baillie
                                  17, 447
PRIOR, Arthur Norman, 1914–69
By A. J. P. Kenny   56, 321
PURSER, Louis Claude, 1854–1932
By A. C. Clark   18, 407

R

RADCLIFFE-BROWN, Alfred Reginald,
1881–1955
By Sir R. W. Firth   42, 287
RAMSAY, Sir James Henry, 1832–1925
By T. F. Tout   11, 479
RANDLE, Herbert Niel, 1880–1973
By T. Burrow   60, 431
RAPSON, Edward James, 1861–1937
By L. D. Barnett   23, 526
RAVEN, Revd. Charles Earle, 1885–
1964
By I. T. Ramsey   51, 467
READ, Sir Charles Hercules, 1857–
1929
By O. M. Dalton   15, 519
REAY, Lord (Donald James Mackay),
1839–1921
By Viscount Bryce   10, 533
REID, James Smith, 1846–1926
By A. Souter, A. C. Clark, and Sir
F. E. Adcock   13, 335
RENWICK, William Lindsay, 1889–
1970
By Winifred Maynard   57, 477
RICHARDSON, Henry Gerald, 1884–
1974
By G. O. Sayles   61, 497
RICHMOND, Admiral Sir Herbert Wil-
liam, 1871–1946
By G. M. Trevelyan   32, 325
RICHMOND, Sir Ian Archibald, 1902–65
By E. Birley   52, 293
RIDGEWAY, Sir William, 1853–1926
By R. S. Conway   12, 327
ROBERTSON, Sir Dennis Holme, 1890–
1963
By Sir J. Hicks   50, 305

ROBERTSON, Donald Struan, 1885–1961
By F. H. Sandbach   48, 411
ROBERTSON, John George, 1867–1933
By G. P. Gooch   19, 360
ROBINSON, Sir Edward Stanley Gotch, 1887–1976
By C. H. V. Sutherland   63, 423
ROBINSON, The Very Revd. Joseph Armitage, 1858–1933
By Revd. J. M. Creed   20, 297
ROSE, Herbert Jennings, 1883–1961
By W. L. Lorimer   48, 397
ROSEBURY, Earl of, 1847–1929
By J. Buchan   16, 392
ROSS, Sir William David, 1877–1971
By Sir G. N. Clark   57, 525
ROSTOVTZEFF, Michael Ivanovitch, 1870–1952
By A. H. M. Jones   38, 347
ROTH, Leon, 1896–1963
By T. E. Jessop   50, 317
ROWLEY, Revd. Harold Henry, 1890–1969
By Revd. G. W. Anderson   56, 309
ROYCE, Josiah, 1855–1916
By W. R. Sorley   7, 585
RUSSELL, Leonard James, 1884–1971
By W. C. Kneale   57, 513

S

SAINTSBURY, George Edward Bateman, 1845–1933
By O. Elton   19, 325
SALISBURY, Bishop of
see Wordsworth, John
SALMON, Revd. George
By the Very Revd. J. H. Bernard   1, 311
SALTER, Revd. Herbert Edward, 1863–1951
By W. A. Pantin   40, 219
SANDYS, Sir John Edwin, 1844–1922
By J. S. Reid   10, 545
SCHILLER, Ferdinand Canning Scott, 1864–1937
By R. R. Marett   23, 538

SCHOLDERER, Victor, 1880–1971
By Sir F. Francis   58, 429
SCOTT, William Robert, 1868–1940
By Sir J. H. Clapham   26, 479
SETON-WATSON, Robert William, 1879–1951
By G. H. Bolsover   37, 343
SHAND, Alexander Faulkner, 1858–1936
By G. F. Stout   22, 401
SHAW, William Arthur, 1865–1943
By Sir J. H. Clapham   29, 349
SIDGWICK, Henry,
By Viscount Bryce   1, 271
SISAM, Kenneth, 1887–1971
By N. R. Ker   58, 409
SLATER, David Ansell, 1866–1938
By H. W. Garrod   25, 339
SMITH, Arthur Hamilton, 1860–1941
By Sir F. G. Kenyon   27, 393
SMITH, David Nichol, 1875–1962
By J. R. Sutherland   48, 449
SMITH, The Very Revd. Sir George Adam, 1856–1942
By S. A. Cook   28, 325
SMITH, George Charles Moore, 1858–1940
By J. Dover Wilson   30, 361
SMITH, Norman Kemp, 1872–1958
By A. C. Ewing   45, 297
SORLEY, William Ritchie, 1855–1935
By Revd. F. R. Tennant   21, 393
SOUTER, Alexander, 1873–1949
By R. J. Getty   38, 255
STAMP, Josiah Charles, Lord, 1880–1941
By Sir J. H. Clapham   27, 453
STEIN, Sir Aurel, 1862–1943
By C. E. A. W. Oldham   29, 329
STENTON, Doris Mary (Lady Stenton), 1894–1972
By Kathleen Major   58, 525
STENTON, Sir Frank Merry, 1880–1967
By (Lady) Doris M. Stenton   54, 315
STEPHEN, Sir Leslie
By F. W. Maitland   1, 316
STOKES, Whitley, 1830–1909
By K. Meyer   4, 363

STOUT, George Frederick, 1860–1944
By C. A. Mace **31**, 307
SUMNER, Benedict Humphrey, 1893–1951
By Sir C. K. Webster **37**, 359
SYKES, The Very Revd. Norman, 1897–1961
By Revd. Canon J. S. Bezzant **47**, 417

T

TAIT, James, 1863–1944
By Sir F. M. Powicke **30**, 379
TARN, Sir William Woodthorpe, 1869–1957
By Sir F. E. Adcock **44**, 253
TAWNEY, Richard Henry, 1880–1962
By T. S. Ashton **48**, 461
TAYLOR, Alfred Edward, 1869–1945
By Sir W. D. Ross **31**, 407
TAYLOR, Revd. Vincent, 1887–1968
By Revd. C. K. Barrett **56**, 283
TEMPERLEY, Harold William Vazeille, 1879–1939
By G. P. Gooch **25**, 355
TEMPLE, Sir Richard Carnac, Bt., 1850–1931
By R. E. Enthoven (signed R. E. E.) **17**, 393
TENNANT, Revd. Frederick Robert, 1866–1957
By C. D. Broad **44**, 241
THOMAS, David Winton, 1901–70
By Sir G. R. Driver **57**, 463
THOMAS, Frederick William, 1867–1956
By H. N. Randle **44**, 207
THOMAS, Sir Henry, 1878–1952
By V. Scholderer **40**, 241
THOMPSON, Alexander Hamilton, 1873–1952
By D. Douglas **38**, 317
THOMPSON, Sir Edward Maunde, 1840–1929
By Sir F. G. Kenyon **15**, 477
THOMPSON, Revd. James Matthew, 1878–1956
By A. Goodwin **43**, 271

THOMPSON, Reginald Campbell, 1876–1941
By Sir G. R. Driver **30**, 447
TILLOTSON, Geoffrey, 1905–69
By Mary M. Lascelles **56**, 351
TILLYARD, Eustace Mandeville Wetenhall, 1889–1962
By B. Willey **49**, 387
TITMUSS, Richard Morris, 1907–73
By Margaret Gowing **61**, 401
TOD, Marcus Niebuhr, 1878–1974
By R. Meiggs **60**, 485
TOUT, Thomas Frederick, 1855–1929
By Sir F. M. Powicke **15**, 491
TOYNBEE, Arnold Joseph, 1889–1975
By W. H. McNeill **63**, 441
TOYNBEE, Paget, 1855–1932
By E. G. Gardner **18**, 441
TOZER, Revd. Henry Fanshawe, 1829–1916
By W. W. Jackson **7**, 566
TREVELYAN, George Macauley, 1876–1962
By Sir G. N. Clark **49**, 375
TREVELYAN, Sir George Otto, 1838–1928
By B. Williams **16**, 383
TURNER, George James, 1867–1946
By Sir C. T. Carr **40**, 207
TYRRELL, Robert Yelverton, 1844–1914
By L. C. Purser **7**, 533

V

VINOGRADOFF, Sir Paul, 1854–1925
By Sir W. S. Holdsworth **11**, 486

W

WACE, Alan John Bayard, 1879–1957
By F. H. Stubbings **44**, 263
WADE-GERY, Henry Theodore, 1888–1972
By A. Andrewes **59**, 419
WAISMANN, Friedrich, 1896–1959
By S. N. Hampshire **46**, 309

WALKER, John, 1900–64
By Sir E. S. G. Robinson   **52**, 287
WALPOLE, Sir Spencer, 1839–1907
By Sir A. C. Lyall   **3**, 373
WARD, Sir Adolphus William, 1837–1924
By T. F. Tout   **11**, 427
WARD, James, 1843–1925
By W. R. Sorley   **12**, 306
WARNER, Sir George Frederick, 1845–1936
By Sir F. G. Kenyon   **22**, 345
WEBB, Beatrice, 1858–1943
By R. H. Tawney   **29**, 285
WEBB, Clement Charles Julian, 1865–1954
By Sir W. D. Ross   **41**, 339
WEBB, Geoffrey Fairbank, 1898–1970
By Margaret D. Whinney   **57**, 453
WEBSTER, Sir Charles Kingsley, 1886–1961
By S. T. Bindoff and Sir G. N. Clark   **48**, 427
WEBSTER, Mrs. Madge
see Dale, Amy Marjorie
WELLESZ, Egon J., 1885–1974
By W. F. Oakeshott   **61**, 567
WESTRUP, Sir Jack Allan, 1904–75
By G. Abraham   **63**, 471
WHEELER, Sir Robert Eric Mortimer, 1890–1976
By Jacquetta Hawkes   **63**, 483
WHITE, The Very Revd. Henry Julian, 1859–1934
By S. C. E. Legg   **22**, 408
WHITEHEAD, Alfred North, 1861–1947
By Dorothy Emmet   **33**, 293

WILLIAMS, Basil, 1867–1950
By R. Pares   **36**, 251
WILLIAMS, Sir Harold Herbert, 1880–1964
By G. Tillotson   **51**, 455
WILLIAMS, Sir Ifor, 1881–1965
By I. Ll. Foster   **53**, 361
WILSON, Frank Percy, 1889–1963
By H. Davis   **49**, 441
WILSON, John Cook, 1849–1915
By H. W. B. Joseph   **7**, 555
WILSON, John Dover, 1881–1969
By H. Jenkins   **59**, 383
WINFIELD, Sir Percy Henry, 1878–1953
By S. J. Bailey   **41**, 329
WOODWARD, Sir Ernest Llewellyn, 1890–1971
By R. Butler   **57**, 497
WORDSWORTH, The Rt. Revd. John (Bishop of Salisbury, 1885–1911), 1843–1911
By Revd. W. Sanday   **5**, 530
WORMALD, Francis, 1904–72
By A. J. Brown   **61**, 523
WRIGHT, Joseph, 1855–1930
By Sir C. H. Firth   **18**, 423
WRIGHT, Robert Alderston, Lord, 1869–1964
By A. L. Goodhart   **51**, 429

Z

ZETLAND, Lawrence John Lumley Dundas, Marquess of, 1876–1961
By Sir G. Laithwaite   **47**, 387

INDEX OF TITLES
AND SUBJECTS

A

ABBO OF FLEURY'S *QUAESTIONES GRAMMATICALES*, ON THE TEXT OF
By H. Bradley   10, 173

ABSOLUTE IDEALISM (DH)
By A. M. Quinton   57, 303

ACADEM ROIAL OF KING JAMES I, THE
By Ethel M. Portal   7, 189

ACADEMIC FREEDOM, OF (TOB)
By Lord Robbins   52, 45

ACADEMIC PROFESSION, THE (TOB)
By Sir E. Ashby   55, 163

ACADEMY
see British Academy

ACTIVITY AND DESCRIPTION IN ARISTOTLE AND THE STOA (DH)
By A. C. Lloyd   56, 227

AESCHYLUS: NEW TEXTS AND OLD PROBLEMS
By E. Fraenkel   28, 237

AESTHETIC APPRECIATION OF BELGIUM'S PAST, AN (AC)
By E. Verhaeren   8, 81

AFRICA, SOUTH
Lord Milner and South Africa (R)
By E. A. Walker   28, 155

AFRICAN TRADITIONAL LAW IN HISTORICAL PERSPECTIVE (RB)
By M. Gluckman   60, 295

AGE AND AUTHORITY IN EARLY MODERN ENGLAND (R)
By Keith Thomas   62, 205

AGE OF TENNYSON, THE (W)
By G. M. Young   25, 125

AÏ KHANUM ON THE OXUS: A HELLENISTIC CITY IN CENTRAL ASIA (AR)
By P. Bernard   53, 71

ALBERTI, LEON BATTISTA, AND THE BEGINNINGS OF ITALIAN GRAMMAR (I)
By C. Grayson   49, 291

ALBERTI, LEON BATTISTA, ON PAINTING (I)
By Lord Clark   30, 283

ALEXANDER THE GREAT AND THE UNITY OF MANKIND (R)
By Sir W. W. Tarn   19, 123

ALEXANDRIAN FORGERIES, SOME
By P. M. Fraser   47, 243

'ALĪ B. RABBAN'S BOOK OF RELIGION AND EMPIRE
By D. S. Margoliouth   16, 165

ALLEGORISTS, SPENSER AND THE (W)
By J. F. Kermode   48, 261

'ALPAMYSH', THE EPIC OF, AND THE RETURN OF ODYSSEUS
By Y. Zhirmunsky   52, 267

AMBIGUITY OF THE WORD 'GOOD', AN (P)
By E. F. Carritt   23, 51

AMERICAN HISTORY
The Debate on the American Civil War (STP). By Sir D. Brogan   49, 203
Violence in American Society (STP). By H. G. Nicholas   55, 145
The Discovery of America and the Discovery of Man (R). By J. H. Elliot   58, 67
The End of British Administration in the North American Colonies (STP). By K. G. Davies   61, 131

AMERICAN LITERATURE
The Sound of American Literature a Century Ago (STP). By C. Bode   47, 97

AMERICAN LITERATURE (*cont.*):
Literature and Education in the United States (STP). By D. Daiches   **51**, 357
Nationalism and the Literature of the United States (STP). By D. Grant   **53**, 179
Problems and Roles of the American Artist as Portrayed by the American Novelist (STP). By P. A. Tanner   **57**, 159
Some Aspects of the American Short Story (STP). By W. E. Allen   **59**, 125
The Outland Dart: American Writers and European Modernism (STP). By M. Bradbury   **63**, 33

ANATOLIA, BRONZE AGE ARCHITECTURE (AR)
By Seton Lloyd   **49**, 153

ANATOLIA: ÇATAL HÜYÜK, A NEOLITHIC CITY (AR)
By J. Mellaart   **51**, 201

ANCHORITE, THE BOOK OF THE (JR)
By I. Ll. Foster   **36**, 197

ANCIENT COINAGE OF SOUTHERN ARABIA, THE
By Sir G. F. Hill   **7**, 57

ANCIENT GREEK ACCENTUATION, ON
By J. P. Postgate   **11**, 213

ANCRENE WISSE (OR *ANCRENE RIWLE*), THE DATE AND COMPOSITION OF (IG)
By E. J. Dobson   **52**, 181

ANGLES, THE SAXONS, AND THE JUTES, THE (R)
By J. N. L. Myres   **56**, 145

ANGLO-SAXON ILLUMINATION AFTER THE NORMAN CONQUEST (AA)
By F. Wormald   **30**, 127

ANGLO-SAXON, THE LITERATE (IG)
By J. E. Cross   **58**, 67

ANGLO-SAXON ROYAL GENEALOGIES
By K. Sisam   **39**, 287

ANNALES CAMBRIAE AND RELATED TEXTS (JR)
By Kathleen Hughes   **59**, 233

ANTHROPOLOGY
The Sceptical Anthropologist? By Sir R. W. Firth   **58**, 177

ANTHROPOMORPHISM AND PHYSICS (P)
By T. P. Nunn   **13**, 13

APPRECIATION OF SCULPTURE, THE (AA)
By Sir E. Maclagan   **11**, 311

AQUINAS, SAINT THOMAS (MM)
By E. Gilson   **21**, 29

ARA PACIS, THE, RECONSIDERED AND HISTORICAL ART IN ROMAN ITALY (I)
By J. M. C. Toynbee   **39**, 67

ARAB RULE UNDER THE AL BU SA'ID DYNASTY OF OMAN (R)
By Bertram Thomas   **24**, 27

ARABIA AND ARABIC
Some Aspects of Ancient Arabic Poetry. By Sir C. J. Lyall   **8**, 365
Report of the Committee on Arabic Transliteration   **8**, 505
Two South Arabian Inscriptions. By D. S. Margoliouth   **11**, 177
Four Strange Tongues from South Arabia—The Hadara Group. By Bertram Thomas   **23**, 231

ARCHAEOLOGY AND FOLK TRADITION (JR)
By H. J. Fleure   **17**, 369

ARCHAISM OF IRISH TRADITION, THE (JR)
By M. Dillon   **33**, 245

ARCHBISHOP THOMAS BECKET: A CHARACTER STUDY (R)
By Revd. M. D. Knowles   **35**, 177

ARISTOTLE (MM)
By J. Burnet   **11**, 109

ARISTOTLE ON *EUDAIMONIA* (DH)
By J. L. Ackrill   **60**, 339

ARISTOTLE, THE PLATONISM OF (DH)
By G. E. L. Owen   **51**, 125

ARISTOTLE AND THE STOA, ACTIVITY AND DESCRIPTION IN (DH)
By A. C. Lloyd   **56**, 227

ARISTOTELIAN LEARNING IN OXFORD
By D. A. Callus   **29**, 229

ARISTOTLE'S THOUGHT, THE DEVELOP-
MENT OF (DH)
By Sir W. D. Ross   43, 63
ARMADA, THE FAILURE OF THE
SPANISH
By J. H. Rose   22, 207
ARMOUR, THE ETCHED DECORATION
OF (AA)
By Sir J. G. Mann   28, 17
ARNOLD, MATTHEW (W)
By Sir E. K. Chambers   18, 23
ARNOLD, MATTHEW, AND CARLYLE
(W)
By Kathleen Tillotson   42, 133
ART IN ENGLAND, 1800–1920 (AA)
By Sir R. Blomfield   9, 375
ART OF GEOFFREY CHAUCER, THE (IG)
By J. L. Lowes   16, 297
ART OF THE NORTHERN NOMADS, THE
(AA)
By Sir E. H. Minns   28, 47
ART OF PRINTING, THE (AA)
By S. Morison   23, 373
ART OF THE SEVERAN AGE IN THE
LIGHT OF TRIPOLITANIAN DIS-
COVERIES, THE
By J. B. Ward Perkins   37, 269
ARTEMIS EPHESIA
By D. G. Hogarth   2, 375
ARTHURIAN LEGENDS (THE 'MATIÈRE
DE BRETAGNE') IN ITALY, NOTES
ON
By E. G. Gardner   15, 179
ARTISTIC CREATION AND COSMIC CREA-
TION (P)
By S. Alexander   13, 247
ASIA MINOR
Excavation in Asia Minor. By Sir
W. M. Ramsay   1, 109
Artemis Ephesia. By D. G. Hogarth
2, 375
The Intermixture of Races in Asia
Minor. By Sir W. M. Ramsay
7, 359
ASPECTS OF CELTIC MYTHOLOGY (JR)
By A. G. van Hamel   20, 207
ASPECTS OF CLASSICAL LEGEND AND
HISTORY IN SHAKESPEARE (S)
By F. S. Boas   29, 107

ASSYRIAN TABLETS FROM SULTANTEPE,
THE
By O. R. Gurney   41, 21
ATTEMPT TO RECOVER THE ORIGINAL
ORDER OF THE TEXT OF REVELA-
TION, XX.4–XXII, AN
By the Ven. C. H. Charles   7, 37
ATTIC BLACK-FIGURE (AA)
By Sir J. D. Beazley   14, 217
ATTIC TRAGEDY, THE STRUCTURE OF
STICHOMYTHIA IN
By Sir J. L. Myres   34, 199
ATTIC VASES IN THE CYPRUS MUSEUM
By Sir J. D. Beazley   33, 195
AUSTRALIAN ABORIGINES
The Origin of Terms of Human
Relationship. By A. Lang
3, 139

B

BACCHIC ELEMENT IN SHAKESPEARE'S
PLAYS, THE (S)
By E. Legouis   12, 115
BACCHYLIDES
By Sir R. C. Jebb   1, 203
BACON, FRANCIS
Palissy, Bacon, and the Revival of
Natural Science. By Sir T. C.
Allbutt   6, 233
BACON, FRANCIS (MM)
By A. E. Taylor   12, 273
BACON, ROGER
By Sir J. E. Sandys   6, 371
BACON, ROGER (MM)
By A. G. Little   14, 265
BACTRIA
Aï Khanum on the Oxus (AR). By
P. Bernard   53, 71
BAGEHOT, WALTER (MM)
By Sir K. C. Wheare   60, 173
BALLADS, THE HISTORY OF, 1100–
1500
By W. P. Ker   4, 179
BAROQUE ART (AA)
By G. Webb   33, 131
BAROQUE CHARACTER OF THE ELIZA-
BETHAN TRAGIC HERO, THE (S)
By L. L. Schücking   24, 85

BAROQUE AND ROCOCO: SOME USES
    AND MISUSES OF THE TERMS
By A. Blunt   58, 215
BASIS OF REALISM, THE
By S. Alexander   6, 279
BEARING OF THE 'CURSUS' ON THE TEXT
    OF DANTE'S 'DE VULGARI ELO-
    QUENTIA', THE
By P. Toynbee   10, 359
BECKET, ARCHBISHOP THOMAS: A
    CHARACTER STUDY (R)
By Revd. M. D. Knowles   35, 177
BEDE (MM)
By R. W. Chambers   22, 129
BEDE, THE OLD ENGLISH (IG)
By Dorothy Whitelock   48, 57
BEETHOVEN (MM)
By Sir W. H. Hadow   8, 135
BEGINNING OF THE YEAR IN THE
    MIDDLE AGES, THE
By R. L Poole   10, 113
BEGINNINGS OF A MODERN CAPITAL
    THE (R)
By T. F. Tout   10, 487
BELGIUM'S PAST. AN AESTHETIC AP-
    PRECIATION (AC)
By E. Verhaeren   8, 81
BÉMONT, CHARLES, AND HIS SERVICES
    TO ENGLISH HISTORY
By E. F. Jacob   25, 301
BENEDICT IX AND GREGORY VI
By R. L. Poole   8, 199
BENTHAM (MM)
By H. L. A. Hart   48, 297
BENTHAM, JEREMY, AND THE GREEK
    INDEPENDENCE (Ex.A)
By Pan. J. Zepos   62, 293
BENTLEY'S MILTON (W)
By J. W. Mackail   11, 55
BEOWULF: THE MONSTERS AND THE
    CRITICS (IG)
By J. R. R. Tolkien   22, 245
BERGSON, H.
    'Time' and 'History' in Contem-
    porary Philosophy
By H. W. Carr   8, 331
BERGSON ON MORALITY (DH)
By Revd. F. C. Copleston,   41, 247

BERKELEY'S   ARGUMENT   ABOUT
    MATERIAL SUBSTANCE (P)
By C. D. Broad   28, 119
BERKELEY'S SIRIS, GEORGE: THE PHILO-
    SOPHY OF THE GREAT CHAIN OF
    BEING AND THE ALCHEMICAL
    THEORY (P)
By A. D. Ritchie   40, 41
BIRTH OF THE DUTCH REPUBLIC, THE
    (R)
By Sir G. N. Clark   32, 189
BLACK BOOK OF CAMARTHEN, THE.
    'STANZAS OF THE GRAVES' (JR)
By Thomas Jones   53, 97
BLASON DE LA FRANCE, LE (AC)
By M. Barrès   7, 339
BOCCACCIO
    Some Aspects of the Genius of
    Giovanni Boccaccio (I). By E.
    Hutton   10, 219
BOOK OF THE ANCHORITE, THE (JR)
By I. Ll. Foster   36, 197
'THE BOOK OF RELIGION AND EMPIRE'
    BY 'ALĪ B. RABBAN AL-TABARI,
    ON
By D. S. Margoliouth   16, 165
BOSNIA, ROLE IN INTERNATIONAL POLI-
    TICS (1875–1914) (R)
By R. W. Seton-Watson   17, 335
BOUNDARY LINE OF CYMRU, THE (JR)
By Sir C. Fox   26, 275
BRADLEY, MR F. H., THE META-
    PHYSIC OF
By the Very Revd. H. Rashdall
                               5, 429
BRETONS ET ANGLAIS AUX Vᵉ ET VIᵉ
    SIÈCLES (JR)
By F. Lot   16, 327
BRITAIN AND JULIUS CÆSAR (MW)
By C. F. C. Hawkes   63, 125
BRITISH ACADEMY
    A Brief Account of the Foundation
    of the Academy   1, vii
    Charter of Incorporation   1, x
    Bye-Laws   1, xiv
    See Presidential Addresses
BRITISH CHARACTER, THE: THE LION
    AND THE OSTRICH (TOB) 59, 189
By A. Koestler

BRITISH CONTRIBUTION TO THE NEO-
CLASSICAL STYLE IN PAINTING (AA)
By Sir E. K. Waterhouse   **40**, 57
BRITISH FOREIGN POLICY SINCE 1945
(TOB)
By Roy Jenkins   **58**, 153
BRITISH MERCHANTS AND SOUTH
AMERICAN INDEPENDENCE (R)
By R. A. Humphreys   **51**, 151
BRITISH SCHOOL OF MINIATURE POR-
TRAIT-PAINTERS, THE (AA)
By C. Winter   **34**, 119
BRITISH SOLDIER AND THE EMPIRE,
THE (R)
By the Hon. Sir J. Fortescue
9, 409
BRITTANY, THE COLONISATION FROM
CELTIC BRITAIN (JR)
By Norah K. Chadwick   **51**, 235
BRONZE AGE ARCHITECTURE OF ANA-
TOLIA (AR)
By Seton Lloyd   **49**, 153
BROWNING, ROBERT (W)
By I. Jack   **53**, 219
BROWNING'S LYRICISM (W)
By Rachel Trickett   **57**, 65
BULGARIAN AND OTHER ATROCITIES,
THE, 1875–8
By H. W. V. Temperley   **17**, 105
BURIDAN, JOHN AND SOME PROBLEMS
OF SELF-REFERENCE (DH)
By A. N. Prior   **48**, 281
BURKE (MM)
By G. M. Young   **29**, 19
BURNS AND THE PEASANTRY 1785 (W)
By Revd. J. Kinsley   **60**, 135
BYRD, WILLIAM, 1623–1923 (AA)
By Sir W. H. Hadow   **10**, 395
BYRON, LORD: ARNOLD AND SWIN-
BURNE (W)
By Sir H. J. C. Grierson   **9**, 431
BYRON, LORD, THE POETRY OF (W)
By J. Buxton   **56**, 77
BYRON AS POET (C)
By W. W. Robson   **43**, 25
BYZANTINE ASTROLABE AT BRESCIA,
THE
By O. M. DALTON   **12**, 133

C

CABINET COUNCIL, THE, 1783–1835
(R)
By A. Aspinall   **38**, 145
CÆDMON, THE POETRY OF (IG)
By C. L. Wrenn   **32**, 277
CAMARTHEN, THE BLACK BOOK OF
(JR)
By Thomas Jones   **53**, 97
CAMDEN, WILLIAM, AND THE BRITAN-
NIA (AR)
By S. Piggott   **37**, 199
CAN REASON BE PRACTICAL? (P)
By H. J. Paton   **29**, 65
CAPELL, EDWARD, AND HIS EDITION OF
SHAKESPEARE (S)
By Alice Walker   **46**, 131
CARCHEMISH, HITTITE PROBLEMS AND
THE EXCAVATION OF
By D. G. Hogarth   **5**, 361
CARCHEMISH, DATE OF THE HITTITE
HIEROGLYPHIC INSCRIPTIONS
By Sir A. E. Cowley   **14**, 39
CARDINAL POLE'S MANUSCRIPTS
By E. Lobel   **17**, 97
CARLAVEROCK, THE SONG OF, AND THE
PARLIAMENTARY ROLL OF ARMS
By N. Denholm-Young   **47**, 251
CARLYLE, THOMAS (MM)
By Sir H. J. C. Grierson   **26**, 301
CARLYLE, MATTHEW ARNOLD AND
By Kathleen Tillotson   **42**, 133
CARVING TRIFLES: WILLIAM KING'S
IMITATION OF HORACE (C)
By J. Fuller   **62**, 269
CASSIODORUS AND ITALIAN CULTURE
OF HIS TIME (I)
By A. Momigliano   **41**, 207
CASTLE-BUILDING IN THIRTEENTH-
CENTURY WALES AND SAVOY (AR)
By A. J. Taylor   **63**, 265
ÇATAL HÜYÜK, A NEOLITHIC CITY IN
ANATOLIA (AR)
By J. Mellaart   **51**, 201
CAUSES OF THE BREAK-UP OF THE
MYCENAEAN REGIME IN CYPRUS,
THE
By Sir J. L. Myres   **10**, 355

CELTAE AND GALLI
By Sir J. Rhŷs   2, 71

CELTIC ART
Imagery in Early Celtic Art (JR).
By P. Jacobsthal   27, 301

CELTIC CULTURE, AN EARLY PHASE (JR)
By J. M. de Navarro   22, 297

CELTIC EPIGRAPHY, GLEANINGS IN THE ITALIAN FIELD OF
By Sir J. Rhŷs   6, 315

CELTIC INSCRIPTIONS OF CISALPINE GAUL, THE
By Sir J. Rhŷs   6, 23

CELTIC INSCRIPTIONS OF FRANCE AND ITALY
By Sir J. Rhŷs   2, 273

CELTIC INSCRIPTIONS OF GAUL, THE, Additions and Corrections
By Sir J. Rhŷs   5, 261

CELTIC MYTHOLOGY, ASPECTS OF (JR)
By A. G. van Hamel   20, 207

CELTIC WAVES IN SPAIN, TWO (JR)
By P. Bosch-Gimpera   26, 25

CELTIQUE, LA POSITION LINGUISTIQUE DU (JR)
By J. Vendryes   23, 333

CENSORSHIP AND THE LIMITS OF PERMISSION (TOB)
By J. Miller   57, 281

CENSURED OPINIONS OF UTHRED OF BOLTON, THE
By Revd. M. D. Knowles   37, 305

CENTENARY OF THE FRENCH CIVIL CODE, THE
By Sir C. Ilbert   1, 253

CENTENARY OF KANT'S DEATH, THE
By S. H. Hodgson   1, 169

CENTURY OF DIVINE SONGS, THE (W)
By G. Sampson   29, 37

CERTITUDE ET VÉRITÉ (P)
By E. Boutroux   6, 481

CERVANTES AND SHAKESPEARE (MM)
By J. Fitzmaurice-Kelly   7, 297

CERVANTES IN ENGLAND
By J. Fitzmaurice-Kelly   2, 11

CHANGES IN STANDARDS OF COMFORT IN EIGHTEENTH CENTURY ENGLAND (R)
By T. S. Ashton   41, 171

CHANGING VIEWS OF THE MIND IN ENGLISH POETRY (W)
By G. Bullough   41, 61

CHARACTER AND HISTORY OF PELAGIUS' COMMENTARY ON THE EPISTLES OF ST. PAUL, THE
By A. Souter   7, 261

CHARACTER OF SHAKESPEARE, THE (S)
By the Very Revd. H. C. Beeching   8, 157

CHATTERTON (W)
By W. M. Dixon   16, 183

CHAUCER: SOME REFLECTIONS ON HIS 'ART POETICAL' (IG)
By Dorothy Everett   36, 131

CHAUCER AND THE RHETORICIANS (W)
By J. M. Manly   12, 95

CHAUCER, GEOFFREY: THE ART OF (IG
By J. L. Lowes   16, 297

CHAUCERIAN POETIC, TOWARDS A (IG)
By D. Brewer   60, 219

CHICHESTER; REYNOLD PECOCK, BISHOP OF (R)
By E. F. Jacob   37, 121

CHINESE ART AND BUDDHISM (AA)
By L. Binyon   22, 157

CHRISTIAN DOCUMENTS FROM NUBIA
By F. Ll. Griffith   14, 117

CICERO (MM)
By T. Frank   18, 111

CITY OF LONDON, THE, AND THE DEVONSHIRE-PITT ADMINISTRATION 1756–7 (R)
By Dame Lucy S. Sutherland   46, 147

CIVIL SERVICE, THE ROLE AND CHARACTER OF THE (TOB)
By Sir W. Armstrong   56, 209

CLASSICAL RESEARCH, FLAWS IN
By J. P. Postgate   3, 161

CODEX, THE
By C. H. Roberts   40, 169

COINS
The Earliest Coins of Greece Proper.
By P. Gardner   5, 161

The Ancient Coinage of Southern Arabia. By Sir G. F. Hill   7, 57

The Silver Coinage of Crete. By Sir G. MacDonald   9, 289

The Date of the Roman Denarius and other Landmarks in Early Roman Coinage. By H. Mattingly and Sir E. S. G. Robinson   18, 211

The Imperial 'Vota'. By H. Mattingly   36, 155

The Imperial 'Vota', 2nd part. By H. Mattingly   37, 219

Some New Studies of the Roman Republican Coinage. By H. Mattingly   39, 239

Roman Numismatics: Miscellaneous Notes. By H. Mattingly   43, 179

Roman Numismatics: Further Miscellaneous Notes. By H. Mattingly   46, 249

Various Numismatic Notes. By H. Mattingly   49, 313

COLERIDGE ON IMAGINATION AND FANCY (W)
By B. Willey   32, 173

COLIGNY CALENDAR, THE
By Sir J. Rhŷs   4, 207

COLLINS, THE POETRY OF (W)
By H. W. Garrod   14, 21

COLLINS, WILLIAM, THE POETRY OF (W)
By A. Johnston   59, 321

COLONISATION OF BRITTANY FROM CELTIC BRITAIN, THE (JR)
By Nora K. Chadwick   51, 235

COLOPHONS AND MARGINALIA OF IRISH SCRIBES, ON THE
By Revd. C. Plummer   12, 11

COLOUR QUESTION IN THE PORTUGUESE EMPIRE, THE, 1415–1825 (R)
By C. R. Boxer   47, 113

COLUMN AND LINE IN THE PENINSULAR WAR
By Sir C. W. C. Oman   4, 321

COMMENT SE FORME UNE NATION: LA SUISSE, SA TERRE ET SON HISTOIRE
By G. de Reynold   8, 427

COMMENTARY OF PELAGIUS ON THE EPISTLE OF ST. PAUL, THE
By A. Souter   2, 409

'COMMON GAELIC': THE EVOLUTION OF THE GOEDELIC LANGUAGES (JR)
By K. Jackson   37, 71

COMMON LAW, THE, IN ENGLAND AND AMERICA (TWO BRANCHES OF THE SAME STREAM) (Mac)
By E. N. Griswold   48, 235

COMMON PRIVILEGES OF POETRY', 'THE (W)
By Winifred Nowottny   52, 61

COMPARISON OF KANT'S IDEALISM WITH THAT OF BERKELEY, A (P)
By H. W. B. Joseph   15, 213

COMPASS-CARD, THE ORIGIN AND DEVELOPMENT OF THE
By S. P. Thompson   6, 179

COMPILATION OF THE *CHRONICA MAJORA* OF MATTHEW PARIS, THE
By Sir F. M. Powicke   30, 147

CONCLAVE OF CLEMENT X (1670), THE
By Baron de Bildt   1, 111

CONCRETE BACKGROUND OF PHILOSOPHY, THE
By L. J. Russell   37, 51

CONDOTTE AND *CONDOTTIERI* IN THE THIRTEENTH CENTURY (I)
By D. P. Waley   61, 337

CONNECTION BETWEEN ANCIENT AND MODERN ROMANCE, THE (W)
By W. J. Courthope   5, 245

CONSIDERATION OF MACAULAY'S COMPARISON OF DANTE AND MILTON, A
By W. J. Courthope   3, 259

CONSTANTINE THE GREAT AND THE CHRISTIAN CHURCH (R)
By N. H. Baynes   15, 341

CO-OPERATION IN SHAKESPEARIAN SCHOLARSHIP (S)
By Allardyce Nicoll   38, 71

COPTIC DOCUMENTS IN GREEK SCRIPT
By W. E. Crum   25, 249

CORINTHIAN VASE, A: Ἑλένης ἀπαίτησις
By Sir J. D. Beazley   43, 233

CORIOLANUS (S)
By A. C. Bradley   5, 457

COSMIC LAW IN ANCIENT THOUGHT
  By J. W. R. Davids   **8**, 279
COSTUMES AND FESTIVALS OF MILANESE
  SOCIETY UNDER SPANISH RULE (I)
  By F. Saxl   **23**, 401
COURT POET IN MEDIEVAL IRELAND,
  THE (JR)
  By J. E. Caerwyn Williams
                          57, 85
COURT POETS OF THE WELSH PRINCES,
  THE (JR)
  By J. Lloyd-Jones   **34**, 167
CRITICISM OF POETRY, THE (W)
  By F. L. Lucas   **19**, 167
CROCE, B.
  'Time' and 'History' in Con-
  temporary Philosophy. By H. W.
  Carr   **8**, 331
  Croce's Aesthetic. By B. Bosanquet
                          9, 261
CULTURAL   SIGNIFICANCE   OF   THE
  INDIAN STATES, THE
  By L. F. R. Williams   **16**, 203
CURTIUS
  Ernst Curtius. By T. Hodgkin
                          2, 31
CYMRU, THE BOUNDARY LINE OF (JR)
  By Sir C. Fox   **26**, 275
CYNEWULF AND HIS POETRY (IG)
  By K. Sisam   **18**, 303
CYPRUS
  The Causes of the Break-up of the
  Mycenaean Régime in Cyprus.
  By Sir J. L. Myres   **10**, 355
CYRIAC OF ANCONA (I)
  By B. Ashmole   **45**, 25

D

DANCING SIVA IN EARLY SOUTH
  INDIAN ART, THE (MW)
  By D. Barrett   **62**, 181
DANES IN ENGLAND, THE (R)
  By Sir F. M. Stenton   **13**, 203
DANTE
  Macaulay's comparison of Dante
  and Milton. By W. J. Courthope
                          3, 259
  The bearing of the 'Cursus' on
  Dante's 'De Vulgari Eloquentia'.
  By P. Toynbee   **10**, 359
  Re-reading the Divine Comedy (I).
  By E. R. Vincent   **31**, 223
DANTE (MM)
  By E. G. Gardner   **10**, 97
DANTE—THE POET (I)
  By C. Foligno   **10**, 81
DANTE'S VISION OF HISTORY (I)
  By W. H. V. Reade   **25**, 187
DARWIN, CHARLES (MM)
  By Sir G. de Beer   **44**, 163
DATE AND COMPOSITION OF ANCRENE
  WISSE, THE (IG)
  By E. J. Dobson   **52**, 181
DATE OF THE FIRST SHAPING OF THE
  CUCHULAINN SAGA, THE
  By Sir W. Ridgeway   **2**, 135
DATE OF THE HITTITE HIEROGLYPHIC
  INSCRIPTIONS OF CARCHEMISH
  By Sir A. E. Cowley   **14**, 39
DATE OF THE ROMAN DENARIUS AND
  OTHER LANDMARKS IN EARLY
  ROMAN COINAGE, THE
  By H. Mattingly and Sir E. S. G.
  Robinson   **18**, 211
DAVID, JACQUES-LOUIS: A PERSONAL
  INTERPRETATION (AA)
  By Anita Brookner   **60**, 155
DEBATE ON THE AMERICAN CIVIL WAR,
  THE (STP)
  By Sir D. Brogan   **49**, 203
DECORATION OF THE SISTINE CHAPEL,
  THE (AA)
  By J. Wilde   **44**, 61
DE LA MARE, WALTER, AND THE
  TRAVELLER (W)
  By Vita Sackville-West   **39**, 23
DELISLE, LÉOPOLD, 1826–1910
  By R. L. Poole   **5**, 203
DESCARTES (MM)
  By S. V. Keeling   **34**, 57
DESCARTES: LEIBNITZ AND, PROOF AND
  ETERNAL TRUTHS (DH)
  By I. Hacking   **59**, 175
DESCRIPTIVISM (P)
  By R. M. Hare   **49**, 115

DEVELOPMENT OF ARISTOTLE'S THOUGHT, THE (DH)
By Sir W. D. Ross 43, 63

DEVELOPMENT OF THE BRITISH LITERARY PORTRAIT UP TO SAMUEL JOHNSON, THE (AA)
By D. Piper 54, 51

DEVELOPMENT OF POLITICAL IDEAS IN ITALY IN THE NINETEENTH CENTURY, THE (I)
By L. Villari 12, 67

DEVONSHIRE-PITT ADMINISTRATION, THE 1756–7 (R)
By Dame Lucy S. Sutherland 46, 147

DICTATION, THE USE OF, IN ANCIENT BOOK-PRODUCTION
By T. C. Skeat 42, 179

DIOCESAN ORGANISATION IN THE MIDDLE AGES: ARCHDEACONS AND RURAL DEANS (R)
By A. Hamilton Thompson 29, 153

DIONYSIAC FRESCO, ON THE, IN THE VILLA DEI MISTERI AT POMPEII
By G. Zuntz 49, 177

DISCOVERY OF AMERICA AND THE DISCOVERY OF MAN, THE (R)
By J. H. Elliot 58, 101

DISINTEGRATION OF SHAKESPEARE, THE (S)
By Sir E. K. Chambers 11, 89

DOCTRINE OF DEGREES IN KNOWLEDGE, TRUTH, AND REALITY, THE
By Viscount Haldane 9, 109

DOCUMENTS OF THE GREAT CHARTER OF 1215, THE
By A. J. Collins 34, 233

DONNE: A LONDON POET (C)
By Barbara Everett 58, 245

DOUGLAS, KEITH: A POET OF THE SECOND WORLD WAR (C)
By G. S. Fraser 42, 89

DRAFT OF MAGNA CARTA, A (1215)
By H. V. Galbraith 53, 345

DRAMATIC MONOLOGUE IN THE VICTORIAN PERIOD, THE (W)
By M. W. MacCallum 11, 265

DRYDEN, JOHN, AND A BRITISH ACADEMY
By O. F. Emerson 10, 45

DURA-EUROPOS, RECENT DISCOVERIES AT (AA)
By M. Rostovtzeff 19, 319

DUTY AND IGNORANCE OF FACT (P)
By H. A. Prichard 18, 67

E

EARLIEST COINS OF GREECE PROPER, THE
By P. Gardner 5, 161

EARLIEST SAINTS' LIVES WRITTEN IN ENGLAND, THE (IG)
By B. Colgrave 44, 35

EARLY CHRISTIAN AND JUDAEAN ART IN MESOPOTAMIA: RECENT DISCOVERIES AT DURA-EUROPOS (AA)
By M. Rostovtzeff 19, 319

EARLY CORRESPONDENCE OF JOHN OF SALISBURY, THE
By R. L. Poole 11, 27

EARLY ENGLISH MAGIC AND MEDICINE
By C. Singer 9, 341

EARLY ITALIAN ENGRAVING (AA)
By A. M. Hind 16, 45

EARLY MAN IN THE SOVIET UNION (AR)
By C. B. M. McBurney 61, 171

EARLY SYRIAC LECTIONARY SYSTEM, THE
By F. C. Burkitt 10, 301

EASTER ISLAND EXPEDITION
By Mrs S. Routledge 8, 133

ECONOMIC APPROACH TO PREHISTORY, THE (AR)
By Grahame Clark 39, 215

EDUCATION
The Ferment in Education on the Continent and in America. By Sir M. E. Sadler 1, 81
Research in the History of Education in England. By A. F. Leach 6, 433

EDWARD I's CASTLE-BUILDING IN
WALES (JR)
By Sir J. G. Edwards 32, 15
EGILL SKALLAGRÍMSSON IN ENGLAND
(IG)
By Gwyn Jones 38, 127
EGYPTIAN LANGUAGE, SOME ASPECTS
OF THE
By Sir A. H. Gardiner 23, 81
1848: THE REVOLUTION OF THE INTEL-
LECTUALS (R)
By Sir L. B. Namier 30, 161
EINION OFFEIRIAD AND A WELSH
METRICAL TREATISE (JR)
By T. Parry 47, 177
ELAMITE PROBLEMS (AR)
By Sir M. Mallowan 55, 255
ʽΕΛΕΝΗΣ ʼΑΠΑΙΤΗΣΙΣ
By Sir J. D. Beazley 43, 233
ELIOT, T. S.: LANGUAGE, SINCERITY
AND THE SELF (C)
By J. Casey 63, 95
ELIZABETHAN POLITICAL SCENE, THE
(R)
By Sir J. E. Neale 34, 97
ELIZABETHAN SHAKESPEARE, THE (S)
By J. Dover Wilson 15, 101
ELIZABETHANS AND THE EMPIRE, THE
(R)
By A. F. Pollard 10, 139
EMERGENCE OF SHAKESPEARE'S
TRAGEDY, THE (S)
By H. V. D. Dyson 36, 69
EMPIRE, THE BRITISH SOLDIER AND
THE (R)
By Hon. Sir J. Fortescue 9, 409
END OF THE ANGLO-NORMAN REALM,
THE (R)
By J. C. HOLT 61, 223
END OF BRITISH ADMINISTRATION IN
THE NORTH AMERICAN COLONIES,
THE (STP)
By K. G. Davies 61, 131
ENFORCEMENT OF MORALS, THE (Mac)
By Lord Devlin 45, 129
ENGLAND AND ITALY (I)
By Senator Visconti di Modrone
18, 135

ENGLISH EPIC TRADITION, THE (W)
By E. M. W. Tillyard 22, 35
ENGLISH HISTORICAL PORTRAIT, THE:
DOCUMENT AND MYTH (AA)
By H. M. Hake 29, 133
ENGLISH ORNAMENT IN THE SEVENTH
AND EIGHTH CENTURIES (AA)
By Sir C. R. Peers 12, 45
ENGLISH PLACE-NAME STUDY
By Sir A. Mawer 10, 31
ENGLISH POETRY IN ITS RELATION TO
PAINTING AND THE OTHER ARTS
(AC)
By L. Binyon 8, 381
ENGLISH PRIMITIVES (AA)
By T. Borenius 11, 75
ENGLISH STAINED GLASS AND GLASS-
PAINTERS IN THE FOURTEENTH
CENTURY (AA)
By Revd. C. Woodforde 25, 29
ENGLISHMEN AND ITALIANS (I)
By G. M. Trevelyan 9, 91
EPIC OF 'ALPAMYSH' AND THE RETURN
OF ODYSSEUS, THE
By V. Zhirmunsky 52, 267
ERASMUS' SERVICES TO LEARNING (MM)
By P. S. Allen 11, 349
ERATOSTHENES OF CYRENE (MM)
By P. M. Fraser 56, 175
ERNST CURTIUS
By T. Hodgkin 2, 31
EROSIONS OF PERSONAL FREEDOM IN
A MODERN SOCIETY (TOB)
By Lord Goodman 54, 133
ETCHED DECORATION OF ARMOUR, THE
(AA)
By Sir J. G. Mann 28, 17
ETHIOPIA
Tiberius and Pontius Pilate in
Ethiopian Tradition and Poetry.
By E. Cerutti 59, 141
EUROPEAN ECONOMIC COMMUNITY, THE
'NON-CONTRACTUAL' LIABILITY
OF THE (Mac)
By Lord Mackenzie Stuart 61, 109
EVIDENCE OF GREEK PAPYRI WITH
REGARD TO TEXTUAL CRITICISM,
THE
By Sir F. G. Kenyon 1, 139

EVOLUTION OF ANCIENT INDIAN ARCHITECTURE, THE
By A. A. MacDonell   **4**, 29

EVOLUTION, THE INTERPRETATION OF
By W. R. Sorley   **4**, 147

EXCAVATION IN ASIA MINOR
By Sir W. M. Ramsay   **1**, 109

EXCAVATIONS AT SURKH KOTAL, THE (AR)
By D. Schlumberger   **47**, 77

F

'FAERIE QUEEN, THE' (W)
By W. L. Renwick   **33**, 149

FALL OF NINEVEH, THE
By C. J. Gadd   **10**, 473

FAMILIAR BELIEFS AND TRANSCENDENT REASON (P)
By Lord Balfour   **11**, 395

FAMILY BREAKDOWN AND SOCIAL POLICY (Mac)
By Lord McGregor   **59**, 65

FELICE FELICIANO *ANTIQUARIUS* (I)
By C. Mitchell   **47**, 197

FERMENT IN EDUCATION ON THE CONTINENT AND IN AMERICA, THE
By Sir M. E. Sadler   **1**, 81

FERRERS, WILLIAM
An Illustrated Letter of Fraternity.
By A. G. Little   **27**, 269

FIGURE IN A LANDSCAPE, THE: WORDSWORTH'S EARLY POETRY (W)
By R. Sharrock   **58**, 313

FINNSBURUH (IG)
By R. Girvan   **26**, 327

FIRE I' THE FLINT, THE: REFLECTIONS ON THE POETRY OF GERARD MANLEY HOPKINS (C)
By S. Heaney   **60**, 413

FIRST REPORT ON RECENT EXCAVATIONS IN ROMAN BRITAIN
By F. J. Haverfield   **4**, 319

FLAVIAN RELIEF IN THE LOUVRE, A
By H. Stuart Jones   **10**, 358

FLAVIO BIONDO AND THE MIDDLE AGES (I)
By D. Hay   **45**, 97

FLAWS IN CLASSICAL RESEARCH
By J. P. POSTGATE   **3**, 161

FORTIFICATION IN ISLAM BEFORE AD 1250 (AA)
By Sir K. A. C. Creswell   **38**, 89

FOSCOLO, UGOLO, THE POETRY OF (I)
By A. Cippico   **11**, 13

FOUNDATION OF SHAKESPEARE'S TEXT, THE (S)
By A. W. Pollard   **10**, 379

FOUR STRANGE TONGUES FROM SOUTH ARABIA—THE HADARA GROUP
By Bertram Thomas   **23**, 231

FOX, CHARLES JAMES, SINCERITY AND INSINCERITY IN (R)
By Sir H. Butterfield   **57**, 237

FRANCE, LE BLAZON DE LA (AC)
By M. Barrès   **7**, 339

FRANCISCAN DOCUMENTS, SOME RECENTLY DISCOVERED
By A. G. Little   **12**, 147

FREE VERSE (W)
By G. Hough   **43**, 157

FREEDOM AND RESENTMENT (P)
By P. F. Strawson   **48**, 187

FRENCH ARCHITECTURE AND STONECARVING IN SOUTHERN FRANCE IN THE TENTH AND ELEVENTH CENTURIES (AA)
By Sir A. W. Clapham   **18**, 47

FRENCH HISTORY IN BRITAIN (R)
By R. C. Cobb   **60**, 271

FRENCH LAW
Centenary of the French Civil Code.
By Sir C. Ilbert   **1**, 253

FRIARS
Introduction of the Observant Friars into England. By A. G. Little   **10**, 455

FROM ALEXANDER BURNES TO FREDERICK ROBERTS: A SURVEY OF IMPERIAL FRONTIER POLICY (R)
By J. L. Morison   **22**, 117

FROM HENRY V TO HAMLET (S)
By H. Granville-Barker   **11**, 283

G

GAELIC STORY-TELLER, THE (JR)
By J. H. Delargy   31, 177
GANDHARA SCULPTURE, THE WESTERN
    ASPECTS OF
By H. Buchtal   31, 151
GAUTAMA THE BUDDHA (MM)
By S. Radhakrishnan   24, 143
GIBBON, EDWARD (MM)
By C. Dawson   20, 159
GLADSTONE AND IRELAND (R)
By J. Vincent   63, 193
GLEANINGS IN THE ITALIAN FIELD OF
    CELTIC EPIGRAPHY
By Sir J. Rhŷs   6, 315
GOEDELIC LANGUAGES, THE EVOLU-
    TION OF THE (JR)
By K. Jackson   37, 71
GOETHE'S CONCEPTION OF FORM (MM)
By Elizabeth M. Wilkinson   37, 175
GOGARTY, OLIVER ST. JOHN (C)
By A. N. Jeffares   46, 73
GOIDELS AND THEIR PREDECESSORS,
    THE (JR)
By T. F. O'Rahilly   21, 323
GOLD COINAGE OF ASIA BEFORE ALEX-
    ANDER THE GREAT, THE
By P. Gardner   3, 107
GOLDEN WORLD OF 'KING LEAR', THE
    (S)
By G. L. Bickersteth   32, 147
GOOD SELF AND THE BAD SELF, THE
    (DH)
By R. Wollheim   61, 373
GRAY, THOMAS: THE POETRY OF (W)
By Lord David Cecil   31, 43
GRAY, THOMAS, THE POETRY OF:
    VERSIONS OF THE SELF (C)
By R. Lonsdale   59, 105
GREAT GAME IN ASIA, THE (1800–
    1844) (R)
By H. W. C. Davis   12, 227
GREAT POETRY (W)
By J. H. A. Sparrow   46, 217
GREEK
    On Ancient Greek Accentuation.
    By J. P. Postgate   11, 213

GREEK ABBREVIATION IN THE
    FIFTEENTH CENTURY
By T. W. Allen   12, 55
GREEK CIVILISATION AS A STUDY FOR
    THE PEOPLE
By W. Rhys Roberts   7, 505
GREEK CRYPTOGRAM, A
By A. S. Hunt   15, 127
GREEK CULTURE OF SOUTH ITALY IN
    THE LATER MIDDLE AGES, THE,
    (I)
By R. Weiss   37, 23
GREEK HISTORICAL DRAMA, A
By E. Lobel   35, 207
GREEK AND MACEDONIAN KINGSHIP
    (R)
By Sir F. E. Adcock   39, 163
GREEK SCULPTURE
    Psychological Elements in Greek
    Sculpture. By P. Gardner   1, 251
    Late Archaic and Early Classical
    Greek Sculpture in Sicily and
    South Italy (AA). By B. Ashmole
                                 20, 91
    Some Nameless Sculptors of the
    Fifth Century BC (AA). By B.
    Ashmole   48, 213
GRENVILLE, SIR RICHARD'S PLACE IN
    ENGLISH HISTORY (R)
By A. L. Rowse   43, 79
GROSSETESTE, ROBERT, AND THE NICO-
    MACHEAN ETHICS
By Sir F. M. Powicke   16, 85
    The 'Notule' of Grosseteste on the
    Nicomachean Ethics. By S. H.
    Thomson   19, 195
GROTIUS, HUGO (MM)
By R. W. Lee   16, 219
'GULLIVER'S TRAVELS': THE POLITICAL
    SIGNIFICANCE OF
By Sir C. H. Firth   9, 237
GYGES; A Greek Historical Drama
By E. Lobel   35, 207

H

HAMLET AND OPHELIA (S)
By Harold Jenkins   49, 135

HAMLET AND ORESTES: A STUDY IN TRADITIONAL TYPES (S)
By G. Murray   6, 389
HAMLET: THE PRINCE OR THE POEM? (S)
By C. S. Lewis   28, 139
HAMMURABI, NEWLY-DISCOVERED LETTERS OF
By S. H. Langdon   10, 357
HARDY, THOMAS: THE LYRICAL POETRY OF (W)
By C. Day Lewis   37, 155
HARRINGTON'S INTERPRETATION OF HIS AGE (R)
By R. H. Tawney   27, 199
HEDONISM AND ART
By L. R. Farnell   14, 99
HEGEL'S LOGIC (DH)
By G. R. G. Mure   44, 21
HENRY I'S PLACE IN ENGLISH HISTORY (R)
By R. W. Southern   48, 127
HERO AND LEANDER (W)
By C. S. Lewis   38, 23
'HIPPOCRATES' AND THE CORPUS HIPPOCRATICUM
By W. H. S. Jones   31, 103
HISTORICAL BACKGROUND OF THE LATER IRISH EPIC, THE (THE CYCLE OF FINN AND OSSIAN)
By Sir W. Ridgeway   4, 343
HISTORICAL CHARACTER OF ENGLISH LYRIC, THE (W)
By G. Saintsbury   5, 475
HISTORICAL STUDIES: THE PRESENT STATE OF (R)
By E. L. Woodward   36, 95
HISTORY AND ART IN THE QUATTROCENTO (I)
By E. Armstrong   10, 415
HISTORY OF THE BALLADS, ON THE, 1100–1500
By W. P. Ker   4, 179
HISTORY, NEGLECTED BRITISH
By Sir W. M. F. Petrie   8, 251
HISTORY, THE STUDY OF, IN GREAT BRITAIN
By T. F. Tout   6, 139

HITLER AND THE ORIGINS OF THE SECOND WORLD WAR (R)
By A. Bullock (Lord Bullock)   53, 259
HITTITE PROBLEMS AND THE EXCAVATION OF CARCHEMISH
By D. G. Hogarth   5, 361
HOBBES, (MM)
By G. P. Gooch   25, 85
HOLLAND
The Birth of the Dutch Republic (R)
By Sir G. N. Clark   32, 189
HOMERIC SCHOLIA, THE
By T. W. Allen   17, 179
HOPKINS, GERARD MANLEY: AN IDIOM OF DESPERATION (C)
By J. Wain   45, 173
HOPKINS, GERARD MANLEY: REFLECTIONS ON THE POETRY OF (C)
By S. Heaney   60, 413
HORACE
By E. Fraenkel   22, 31
HUMAN NATURE AND HUMAN HISTORY
By R. G. Collingwood   22, 97
HUMANISM, THE LIMITS OF SPECULATIVE (P)
By J. Laird   26, 149
HUME
Naturalism in Book One of Hume's Treatise of Human Nature (DH).
By D. Pears   62, 249
HUME'S DOCTRINE OF SPACE (DH)
By C. D. Broad   47, 161
HYMNS IN THE 18TH CENTURY
The Century of Divine Songs (W).
By G. Sampson   29, 37

I

IDEA OF INVENTION, THE (P)
By W. C. Kneale   41, 85
IDEA OF TRUTH IN MANZONI AND LEOPARDI, THE (I)
By K. Foster   53, 243
IDEALISM AND THE THEORY OF KNOWLEDGE
By E. Caird   1, 95
IFS AND CANS (P)
By J. L. Austin   42, 109

ILLUMINATED LETTER OF FRATERNITY, AN
By A. G. Little 27, 269

IMAGERY IN EARLY CELTIC ART (JR)
By P. Jacobsthal 27, 301

IMAGINATION AND THE SELF (P)
By Bernard Williams 52, 105

IMMATERIALISM (P)
By A. A. Luce 30, 19

IMPACT OF STATUTE ON THE LAW OF ENGLAND, THE (Mac)
By Lord Evershed 42, 247

IMPARTIAL SPECTATOR, THE (DH)
By D. D. Raphael 58, 335

IMPERIAL ADMINISTRATIVE SYSTEM IN THE NINTH CENTURY, THE
By J. B. Bury 4, 347

IMPERIAL INFLUENCES ON THE FORMS OF PAPAL DOCUMENTS
By R. L. Poole 8, 237

IMPERIAL STUDIES IN LONDON, THE ORGANISATION OF
By S. Low 5, 491

IMPERIAL 'VOTA', THE
By H. Mattingly 36, 155
2nd part by H. M. Mattingly 37, 219

'IN BRITANNIA' DANS LE MARTYROLOGE HIÉRONYMIEN
By Pére H. Delahaye 17, 289

IN DEFENCE OF OBJECTIVITY (P)
By Mary B. Hesse 58, 275

INDIA
The Great Game in Asia (1800–1844) (R). By H. W. C. Davis 12, 227
The Mogul Empire and the Modern History of Asia. By Sir A. Lyall 2, 183
The Cultural Significance of the Indian States. By L. F. R. Williams 16, 203
From Alexander Burnes to Frederick Roberts (R). By J. L. Morison 22, 177

INDIAN ARCHITECTURE
The Evolution of Ancient Indian Architecture. By A. A. Mac-Donell 4, 29

INDIAN ART
The Dancing Siva in Early South Indian Art (MW). By D. Barrett 62, 181

INFLATION, THE POLITICAL ECONOMY OF (K)
By T. Wilson 61, 291

INFLUENCE OF ENGLISH POETRY UPON THE ROMANTIC REVIVAL ON THE CONTINENT (W)
By C. Vaughan 6, 261

INHERITANCE OF INEQUALITIES, THE: (K)
By J. E. MEADE 59, 355

INTENTION AND UNCERTAINTY (P)
By H. P. Grice 57, 263

INTERMIXTURE OF RACES IN ASIA MINOR, THE
By Sir W. M. Ramsay 7, 359

INTERNATIONAL ASSOCIATION OF ACADEMIES
Report of Second General Assembly 1, 327

INTERNATIONAL MONETARY PROBLEM, THE (K)
By Lord Robbins 58, 293

INTERPENETRATION OF MAN AND NATURE, THE (W)
By Kathleen Coburn 49, 95

INTERPRETATION OF EVOLUTION, THE
By W. R. Sorley 4, 147

INTERPRETATION OF A MENANDER FRAGMENT
By G. Zuntz 42, 209

INTER-RELATION OF THE ACADEMICAL SCIENCES
By S. H. Hodgson 2, 219

INTRODUCTION OF ARISTOTELIAN LEARNING TO OXFORD
By D. A. Callus 29, 229

INTRODUCTION OF THE OBSERVANT FRIARS INTO ENGLAND
By A. G. Little 10, 455

INTRODUCTION OF THE OBSERVANT FRIARS INTO ENGLAND: A BULL OF ALEXANDER VI
By A. G. Little 27, 155

IRELAND

Studies in Early Irish History. By Sir J. Rhŷs   1, 21

The Date of the First Shaping of the Cuchulainn Saga. By Sir W. Ridgeway   2, 135

The Historical Background of the Later Irish Epic (The Cycle of Finn and Ossian). By Sir W. Ridgeway   4, 343

Prolegomena to the study of the Later Irish Bards, 1200–1500. By E. C. Quiggin   5, 89

On the Colophons and Marginalia of Irish Scribes. By Revd. C. Plummer   12, 11

The Native Irish Grammarian (JR). By O. Bergin   24, 205

The Goidels and their Predecessors (JR). By T. F. O'Rahilly   21, 323

The Linguistic and Historical Value of the Irish Law Tracts (JR). By D. A. Binchy   29, 195

The Archaism of Irish Tradition (JR). By M. Dillon   33, 245

Literary Creation and Irish Historical Tradition (JR). By B. Ó Cuív   49, 233

The Court Poet in Medieval Ireland (JR). By J. E. Caerwen Williams   57, 85

Gladstone and Ireland (R). By J. Vincent   63, 193

IRELAND AND MEDIEVAL EUROPE (JR)
By R. Flower   13, 271

IS DIVINE EXISTENCE CREDIBLE? (P)
By N. Kemp Smith   17, 209

IS THERE A POETIC VIEW OF THE WORLD? (W)
By C. H. Herford   7, 423

ITALIAN ELEMENT IN LATE ROMAN AND EARLY MEDIEVAL ARCHITECTURE, THE (I)
By J. B. Ward-Perkins   33, 163

ITALIAN PEOPLE, THE (I)
By Sir R. Rodd   9, 389

ITALIAN PLAQUETTE, THE (AA)
By Sir J. W. Pope-Hennessy   50, 63

ITALIAN PORTRAITURE OF THE FIFTEENTH CENTURY (I)
By Sir G. F. Hill   11, 331

ITALY

The Development of Political Ideas in Italy in the Nineteenth Century (I) By L. Villari   12, 67

Some Fresh Documents concerning the Italian Risorgimento before 1849 (I). By G. F-H. Berkeley   26, 227

Morals and Manners of the Quattrocento (I). By C. M. Ady   28, 179

Some Condottieri of the Trecento (I) By D. M. Bueno de Mesquita   32, 219

Printers and Readers in Italy in the Fifteenth Century (I). By V. Scholderer   35, 25

Alessandro Manzoni (I). By A. P. d'Entrèves   36, 23

The Greek Culture of South Italy in the later Middle Ages (I). By R. Weiss   37, 23

The Ara Pacis Reconsidered and Historical Art in Roman Italy (I). By J. M. C. Toynbee   39, 67

Cassiodorus and Italian Culture of his time, (I). By A. Momigliano   41, 207

Leon Battista Alberti and the Beginnings of Italian Grammar (I). By C. Grayson   49, 291

The Latifundia in Modern Sicilian History (I). By D. Mack Smith   51, 85

Manzoni and the Catholic Revival (I). By C. Dionisetti   59, 341

Condotte and Condottieri in the Thirteenth Century (I). By D. P. Waley   61, 337

Lorenzo de' Medici: the Formation of his Statecraft (I). By N. Rubinstein   63, 71

ITALY'S PROTECTION OF ART TREASURES AND MONUMENTS DURING THE WAR (I)
By Sir F. de Filippi   8, 291

J

Jacob and the Mandrakes
By Sir J. G. Frazer   8, 57
Jacobean Shakespeare and *Measure for Measure*, The (S)
By R. W. Chambers   23, 135
James I, The Academ Roial of King
By Ethel M. Portal   7, 189
Japan and the West in the Mid-Nineteenth Century (R)
By W. G. Beasley   55, 77
Jedonja d'Elephantine: Sa Lettre à Bagohi, Gouverneur de Jérusalem
By A. Van Hoonacker   7, 209
Johnson, Sammuel (MM)
By S. C. Roberts   30, 51
Jones, Inigo, (MM)
By Sir J. Summerson   50, 169
Judex Tarentinus
By E. Jamison   53, 289
Justification of Deduction, The (P)
By M. A. E. Dummett   59, 201

K

Kant, Immanuel
The Centenary of Kant's Death. By S. H. Hodgson   1, 169
Immanuel Kant (P). By J. Ward   10, 237
A Comparison of Kant's Idealism with that of Berkeley (P). By H. W. B. Joseph   15, 213
Kant on Friendship (DH). By H. J. Paton   42, 45
Kant's Moral Theology (DH). By W. H. Walsh   49, 263
Kant's Conception of Freedom (DH). By S. Körner   53, 193
Keats (W)
By E. de Selinourt   10, 59
Keats and Reality (C)
By J. Bayley   48, 91
Kemble, J. M., and Old English Scholarship (IG)
By B. Dickins   25, 51

Keynes, John Maynard: Economist, Author, Statesman (K)
By E. A. G. Robinson   57, 197
Keynes, On Re-reading (K)
By Lord Kahn   60, 361
Kierkegaard's Two Ways (DH)
By P. Gardiner   54, 207
King John and the Courts of Justice (R)
By Lady Stenton   44, 103
King's, William, Imitation of Horace (C)
By J. Fuller   62, 269
Kipling's Verse, Some Aspects of (C)
By A. Rutherford   51, 375
Kition: Mycenaean and Phoenician (MW)
By V. Karageorghis   59, 259
Knight's Fees
By Sir P. Vinogradoff   3, 15
Knowledge
Things and Sensations. By G. F. Stout   2, 169
Some Cardinal Points in Knowledge By S. H. Hodgson   5, 28
The Doctrine of Degrees in Knowledge, Truth and Reality. By Viscount Haldane   9, 109
Our Knowledge of one another (P). By C. C. J. Webb   16, 281
Our Knowledge of Universals (P). By R. I. Aaron   31, 17

L

Language, On the Relations between Spoken and Written
By H. Bradley   6, 211
Language of the Pastons, The (IG)
By N. Davis   40, 119
Language and Poetry in Shakespeare's Early Plays (S)
By Gladys D. Willcock   40, 103
Lapidary Verse (W)
By R. W. Ketton-Cremer   45, 237

LATE ARCHAIC AND EARLY CLASSICAL GREEK SCULPTURE IN SICILY AND SOUTH ITALY (AA)
By B. Ashmole 20, 91
LATIFUNDIA IN MODERN SICILIAN HISTORY, THE (I)
By D. Mack Smith 51, 85
LAW OF NATIONS, ORTHODOXY AND INNOVATION IN THE (Mac)
By C. W. Jenks 57, 215
LAW AND THE REASONABLE MAN, THE (Mac)
By Lord Reid 54, 189
LAY INVESTITURE AND ITS RELATION TO THE CONFLICT OF EMPIRE AND PAPACY (R)
By Z. N. Brooke 25, 217
LEGISLATORS OF MEDIEVAL ENGLAND, THE (R)
By Helen Cam 31, 127
LEIBNITZ AND DESCARTES: PROOF AND ETERNAL TRUTHS (DH)
By I. Hacking 59, 175
LEIBNIZ: SÉS IDÉES SUR l'ORGANISATION DES RELATIONS INTERNATIONALES (MM)
By P. Schrecker 23, 193
LEONARDO DA VINCI (MM)
By Sir C. J. Holmes 9, 53
LEOPARDI AND WORDSWORTH (I)
By G. L. Bickersteth 13, 47
LESSING (MM)
By Sir E. H. Gombrich 43, 133
LETTRE DE JEDONJA D'ÉLÉPHANTINE À BAGOHI, GOUVERNEUR DE JÉRUSALEM
By A. Van Hoonacker 7, 209
LIFE AND ART IN PREHISTORIC THERA (AR)
By Sp. Marinatos 57, 351
LIMBOURGS, THE, AND THE MASTER OF THE BREVIARY OF JEAN SANS PEUR (AA)
By M. Meiss 56, 111
LIMITS OF SPECULATIVE HUMANISM, THE (P)
By J. Laird 26, 149

LINGUISTIC EVIDENCE AND ARCHAEOLOGICAL AND ETHNOLOGICAL FACTS (JR)
By J. Fraser 12, 257
LINGUISTIC AND HISTORICAL VALUE OF THE IRISH LAW TRACTS, THE (JR)
By D. A. Binchy 29, 195
LION AND THE OSTRICH, THE (TOB)
By A. Koestler 59, 189
LITERACY OF THE MEDIEVAL ENGLISH KINGS, THE
By V. H. Galbraith 21, 201
LITERARY CREATION AND IRISH HISTORICAL TRADITION (JR)
By B. Ó Cuív 49, 233
LITERATE ANGLO-SAXON, THE (IG)
By J. E. Cross 58, 67
LITERATURE AND EDUCATION IN THE UNITED STATES (STP)
By D. Daiches 51, 357
LLYWARCH HÊN, THE POEMS OF (JR)
By I. Williams 18, 269
LOCKE, JOHN
John Locke as a Factor in Modern Thought. By A. C. Fraser 1, 221
Locke's Theory of the State. By Sir F. Pollock. 1, 237
John Locke, (MM). By J. Gibson 19, 29
LOGICAL POSITIVISM AND ANALYSIS (P)
By L. Susan Stebbing 19, 53
LONDON
The Beginnings of a Modern Capital (R). By T. F. Tout 10, 487
LONELY PATRIOT, A: FERDINANDO RANALLI (I)
By Sir W. K. Hancock 27, 275
LOST BEGINNING OF MENANDER, MISOUMENOS, THE
By E. G. Turner 63, 315
LUCRETIUS (MM)
By C. Bailey 35, 143
LYRICAL POETRY OF THOMAS HARDY, THE (W)
By C. Day Lewis 37, 155

M

MACAULAY'S COMPARISON OF DANTE AND MILTON
By W. J. Courthope   3, 259

MACHIAVELLI AND THE ELIZABETHANS (I)
By M. Praz   14, 49

MAGIC
Early English Magic and Medicine. By C. Singer   9, 341

MAGICAL TEXTS FROM A BILINGUAL PAPYRUS IN THE BRITISH MUSEUM
By Sir H. I. Bell, A. D. Nock, and H. Thompson   17, 235

MAGNA CARTA
The Documents of the Great Charter of 1215. By A. J. Collins   34, 233
A Draft of Magna Carta (1215). By H. V. Galbraith   53, 345

MAHDIS AND MAHDISM, ON
By D. S. Margoliouth   7, 213

MAIN STREAM OF MUSIC, THE (AA)
By Sir D. Tovey   24, 113

MANDEVILLE, DR BERNARD (MM)
By F. A. Hayek   52, 125

MANNER OF PROCEEDING IN CERTAIN EIGHTEENTH- AND EARLY NINE-TEENTH-CENTURY POEMS, THE (W)
By G. Tillotson   34, 139

MANX GAELIC, THE STUDY OF (JR)
By R. L. Thomson   55, 177

MANZONI, ALESSANDRO (I)
By A. P. d'Entrèves   36, 23

MANZONI AND THE CATHOLIC REVIVAL (I)
By C. Dionisotti   59, 341

MANZONI AND LEOPARDI, THE IDEA OF TRUTH IN (I)
By K. Foster   53, 243

MARCO POLO AND HIS BOOK (I)
By Sir E. D. Ross   20, 181

MARLOWE, CHRISTOPHER: THE PER-FORMANCE OF DR FAUSTUS (C)
By N. Alexander   57, 331

MARSILIUS OF PADUA (I)
By C. W. Previté-Orton   21, 137

MARTYROLOGE HIÉRONYMIEN, LE, 'IN BRITANNIA' DANS
By Pére H. Delahaye   17, 289

MARVELL, ANDREW, SOME THEMES AND VARIATIONS IN THE POETRY OF (W)
By J. B. Leishman   47, 223

MARVELL: A GREAT MASTER OF WORDS (W)
By Elsie Duncan-Jones   61, 267

MASONS' CRAFT IN ENGLAND, THE
By the Ven. W. Cunningham   6, 167

MASTER OF THE BREVIARY OF JEAN SANS PEUR AND THE LIMBOURGS, THE (AA)
By M. Meiss   56, 111

MEANING OF TELEOLOGY, THE
By B. Bosanquet   2, 235

MEASURE FOR MEASURE: THE PLAY AND THE THEMES (S)
By J. C. Maxwell   60, 199

MEDAL, THE: ITS PLACE IN ART (AA)
By Sir G. F. Hill   27, 225

MEDICI, LORENZO DE': THE FORMATION OF HIS STATECRAFT (I)
By N. Rubinstein   63, 71

MEDIEVAL ALLITERATIVE POETRY IN ENGLAND (IG)
By G. SHEPHERD   56, 57

MEDIEVAL HISTORIOGRAPHY, SOME PROBLEMS IN
By G. G. Coulton   18, 155

MEDIEVAL LATIN 'POETICS', THE
By E. Lobel   17, 309

MEDIEVAL PAINTINGS AT WESTMINSTER (AA)
By W. R. Lethaby   13, 123

MEDIEVAL POETRY AND THE FIGURAL VIEW OF REALITY (IG)
By Elizabeth Salter   54, 73

MEDIAEVAL STUDIES IN GREAT BRIT-AIN, THE PRESENT STATE OF
By T. F. Tout   6, 151

MENANDER, INTERPRETATION OF A FRAGMENT
By G. Zuntz   42, 209

MENANDER'S MISOUMENOS: THE LOST BEGINNING
By E. G. Turner   63, 315

Mental Health in Plato's *Republic* (DH)
By A. J. P. Kenny   55, 229
Mesopotamian Communities, from Julian to the Rise of Islam
By J. B. Segal   41, 109
Metamorphosis of Metaphysics, The (P)
By J. Wisdom   47, 37
Metaphysic of Mr F. H. Bradley, The
By the Very Revd. H. Rashdall   5, 429

Metternich
Palmerston, Metternich and the European System, 1830–1841 (R).
By Sir C. K. Webster   20, 125
Meyerstein, E. H. W. 1889–1952 (C)
By L. Butler   41, 141
Michelangelo's Prophets and Sibyls (AA)
By E. Wind   51, 47
Milanese Society under Spanish Rule—Costumes and Festivals (I)
By F. Saxl   23, 401
Mill, John Stuart (MM)
By Bertrand (Earl) Russell   41, 43
Milner, Lord, and South Africa (R)
By E. A. Walker   28, 155
Milton
Tercentenary of the Birth of John Milton. By Sir A. W. Ward   3, 213
Milton as an Historian. By Sir C. H. Firth   3, 227
Macaulay's Comparison of Dante and Milton. By W. J. Courthope   3, 259
Milton in the Eighteenth Century (1701–1750). By E. Dowden   3, 275
Milton as Schoolboy and Schoolmaster. By A. F. Leach   3, 295
Milton's Fame on the Continent. By J. G. Robertson   3, 319
Samson Agonistes and the Hellenic Drama. By Sir R. C. Jebb   3, 341

Milton and Music. By Sir F. Bridge   3, 349
Tercentenary of Milton's Birth. The, Lines by G. Meredith   3, 353
Bentley's Milton (W). By R. L. Poole   11, 55
Thomas Warton and the Early Poems of Milton (W). By L. C. Martin   20, 25
Poets and their Critics: Langland and Milton (W). By R. W. Chambers   27, 109
Milton (MM). By T. S. Eliot   33, 61
Milton, Lost and Regained (C). By J. Beer   50, 143
Mind, The: Changing Views in English Poetry (W)
By G. Bullough   41, 61
Mind of St. Paul, The (MM)
By T. R. Glover   27, 247
Miniature Portrait-painters, The British School of (AA)
By C. Winter   34, 119
Minôan Crete
The Pictographic and Linear Scripts of Minôan Crete. By Sir A. J. Evans   1, 137
Minoan Art (AA). By E. J. Forsdyke   15, 45

Minos the Destroyer rather than the Creator of the so-called 'Minoan' Culture of Cnossus
By Sir W. Ridgeway   4, 97
Modern French History in Britain (R)
By R. C. Cobb   60, 271
Mogul Empire and the Modern History of Asia, The
By Sir A. Lyall   2, 183
Monosyllabism in English (E)
By O. Jespersen   14, 341
Montesquieu
By Sir I. Berlin   41, 267
Moore, G. E., on the Naturalistic Fallacy (DH)
By C. Levy   50, 251

MORAL INTUITION AND THE PRINCIPLE OF SELF-REALIZATION (P)
By C. A. Campbell   **34**, 23

MORAL PRINCIPLES AND INDUCTIVE POLICIES (P)
By R. B. Braithwaite   **36**, 51

MORAL RULES (P)
By J. D. Mabbott   **39**, 97

MORALITY AND ART (P)
By Philippa Foot   **56**, 131

MORALITY, THE RELATIONS OF, TO RELIGION (P)
By W. G. de Burgh   **21**, 75

MORALS AND MANNERS OF THE QUATTROCENTO (I)
By C. M. Ady   **28**, 179

MORE, SIR THOMAS; THE SAGA AND THE MYTH OF (LH)
By R. W. Chambers   **12**, 179

MOZART (MM)
By E. J. Dent   **39**, 181

MUFADDALĪYĀT
Some Aspects of Ancient Arabic Poetry. By Sir C. J. Lyall   **8**, 365

MUNICIPAL HISTORY
The Study of Early Municipal History in England. By J. Tait   **10**, 201

MUSIC
Beethoven (MM). By Sir W. H. Hadow   **8**, 135
William Byrd, 1623–1923 (AA). By Sir W. H. Hadow   **10**, 395
The Main Stream of Music (AA). By Sir D. Tovey   **24**, 113
The Oldest Slavonic Tradition of Byzantine Music. By C. Høeg   **39**, 37
Mozart (MM). By E. J. Dent   **39**, 181
The Nature of Recitative (AA). By Sir J. A. Westrup   **42**, 27
Unexplored Relationships between Early Seventeenth-century Venetian Opera and Contemporary Music in France and England (I). By R. Leppard   **55**, 99

MUSIC OF THE RENAISSANCE IN ITALY (I)
By E. J. Dent   **19**, 293

MYCENAEAN TREASURE, A
By Sir A. J. Evans   **10**, 355

MYTHICAL SORROWS OF SHAKESPEARE, THE (S)
By C. J. Sisson   **20**, 45

MYTHOLOGIC STUDY, THE VALUE AND METHODS OF
By L. R. Farnell   **9**, 37

N

NATIONAL POLICY AND NAVAL STRENGTH XVITH TO XXTH CENTURY (R)
By Sir H. W. Richmond   **10**, 339

NATIONALISM AND THE LITERATURE OF THE UNITED STATES (STP)
By D. Grant   **53**, 179

NATIVE IRISH GRAMMARIAN, THE (JR)
By O. Bergin   **24**, 205

NATUFIAN CULTURE, THE: A MESOLITHIC PEOPLE IN THE NEAR EAST (AR)
By Dorothy A. E. Garrod   **43**, 211

NATURALISM IN BOOK ONE OF HUME'S *TREATISE OF HUMAN NATURE* (DH)
By D. Pears   **62**, 249

NATURALISTIC ETHICS (P)
By W. F. R. Hardie   **33**, 29

NATURE OF ALLITERATIVE POETRY IN LATE MEDIEVAL ENGLAND, THE (IG)
By G. Shepherd   **56**, 57

NATURE OF RECITATIVE, THE (AA)
By Sir J. A. Westrup   **42**, 27

NATURE OF UNIVERSALS AND PROPOSITIONS, THE (P)
By G. F. Stout   **10**, 157

NAVAL PRIZE LAW, Proposed Changes in
By Sir T. E. Holland   **5**, 144

NAVAL STRENGTH AND NATIONAL POLICY, XVITH TO XXTH CENTURY (R)
By Sir H. W. Richmond **10**, 339
NAVE OF WESTMINSTER, THE
By Revd. R. B. Rackham **4**, 33
NEGLECTED BRITISH HISTORY
By Sir W. M. F. Petrie **8**, 251
NEO-CLASSICAL PAINTING: BRITAIN AND (AA)
By Sir E. K. Waterhouse **40**, 57
NEUTRAL DUTIES IN A MARITIME WAR
By Sir T. E. Holland **2**, 55
NEUTRALS
The Rights of Neutrals. By Sir E. Fry **2**, 265
NEW PSALMS FRAGMENT, A
By J. W. B. Barns and G. D. Kilpatrick **43**, 229
NEWGATE GAOL-DELIVERIES
Some Reflections of a Medieval Criminologist (R). By R. B. Pugh **59**, 83
NEWLY-DISCOVERED LETTERS OF HAMMURABI
By S. H. Langdon **10**, 357
NEWTON, SIR ISAAC (MM)
By C. D. Broad **13**, 173
NEXT THIRTY YEARS, THE
Presidential Address. By Viscount Bryce **8**, 1
NINEVEH, THE FALL OF
By C. J. Gadd **10**, 473
NOBLE MOOR, THE (S)
By Dame Helen L. Gardner **41**, 189
'NON-CONTRACTUAL' LIABILITY OF THE EUROPEAN ECONOMIC COMMUNITY, THE (Mac)
By Lord Mackenzie Stuart **61**, 109
NORMANDY: THE END OF THE ANGLO-NORMAN REALM (R)
By J. C. Holt **61**, 223
NORMANDY, THE RISE OF (R)
By D. Douglas **33**, 101
NORMANS AND THE WELSH MARCH, THE (R)
By Sir J. G. Edwards **42**, 155

NOTES ON THE 'MATIERE DE BRETAGNE' IN ITALY
By E. G. Gardner **15**, 179
NOTES ON THE ORGANISATION OF THE MASONS' CRAFT IN ENGLAND
By the Ven. W. Cunningham **6**, 167
'NOTULE' OF GROSSETESTE ON THE NICOMACHEAN ETHICS, THE
By S. H. Thomson **19**, 195
NOWELL, LAURENCE, AND THE DISCOVERY OF ENGLAND IN TUDOR TIMES (IG)
By R. Flower **21**, 47
NUBIA, CHRISTIAN DOCUMENTS FROM
By F. Ll. Griffith **14**, 117
NUMBERED LECTIONS IN OLD ENGLISH POETICAL MSS, THE
By H. Bradley **7**, 165

O

OBJECTIVITY, IN DEFENCE OF (P)
By Mary B. Hesse **58**, 275
OBJECTS OF THE FIVE SENSES, THE (P)
By J. O. Urmson **54**, 117
OBLIGATION AND OBEDIENCE TO LAW (Mac)
By A. H. Campbell **51**, 337
OLD ENGLISH BEDE, THE (IG)
By Dorothy Whitelock **48**, 57
OLDEST SLAVONIC TRADITION OF BYZANTINE MUSIC, THE
By C. Høeg **39**, 37
ORCHERD OF SYON, THE, AND THE ENGLISH MYSTICAL TRADITION (IG)
By Phyllis Hodgson **50**, 229
ORGANISATION OF IMPERIAL STUDIES IN LONDON, THE
By S. Low **5**, 491
ORIENTAL STUDIES IN ENGLAND AND ABROAD
By T. W. Rhys Davids **1**, 18
ORIGEN (MM)
By the Very Revd. W. R. Inge **32**, 123

ORIGIN OF TERMS OF HUMAN RELA-
TIONSHIP, THE
By A. Lang **3**, 139
ORTHODOXY AND INNOVATION IN THE
LAW OF NATIONS (Mac)
By C. W. Jenks **57**, 215
OTHELLO AND COLOUR PREJUDICE (S)
By G. K. Hunter **53**, 139
OUR KNOWLEDGE OF ONE ANOTHER
(P)
By C. C. J. Webb **16**, 281
OUR KNOWLEDGE OF UNIVERSALS (P)
By R. I. Aaron **31**, 17
OUTLAND DART, THE: AMERICAN
WRITERS AND EUROPEAN MODERN-
ISM (STP)
By M. Bradbury **63**, 33
OWEN, WILFRED (C)
By J. Stallworthy **56**, 241
OXFORD MEETING OF THE ACADEMY
Feb. 27. 1923 **10**, 355

P

PAINTING OF ENGLISH LANDSCAPE, ON
THE (AA)
By Sir K. Clark (Lord Clark)
21, 185
PAINTINGS IN WESTMINSTER ABBEY AND
CONTEMPORARY PAINTINGS (AA)
By F. Wormald **35**, 161
PALESTINIAN CULTS IN THE GRAECO-
ROMAN AGE, SOME
By Sir G. F. Hill **5**, 411
PALISSY, BACON, AND THE REVIVAL OF
NATURAL SCIENCE
By Sir T. C. Allbut **6**, 233
PALLADAS AND CHRISTIANITY
By SIR C. M. Bowra **45**, 255
PALMERSTON, METTERNICH, AND THE
EUROPEAN SYSTEM, 1830–1841
(R)
By Sir C. K. Webster **20**, 125
PAPACY
The Conclave of Clement X (1670).
By Baron de Bildt **1**, 111
Benedict IX and Gregory VI. By
R. L. Poole **8**, 199

Imperial Influences on the Form of
Papal Documents. By R. L.
Poole **8**, 237
Lay Investiture and the Conflict of
Empire and Papacy. By Z. N.
Brooke **25**, 217
Introduction of the Observant Friars
into England: a Bull of Alexander
VI. By A. G. Little **27**, 155
PAPYRI
Evidence of Greek Papyri for
Textual Criticism. By Sir F. G.
Kenyon **1**, 139
Magical Texts from a Bilingual
Papyrus in the British Museum.
By Sir H. I. Bell, A. D. Nock and
H. Thompson **17**, 235
The Western Text in the Gospels
and Acts. By Sir F. G. Kenyon
24, 287
Coptic Documents in Greek Script.
By W. E. Crum **25**, 251
PARDON OF PIERS PLOUGHMAN, THE
(IG)
By N. Coghill **30**, 303
PARIS, MATTHEW: THE COMPILATION
OF HIS *CHRONICA MAJORA*
By Sir F. M. Powicke **30**, 147
PARLIAMENT
The Winning of the Initiative by
the House of Commons (R).
By W. Notestein **11**, 125
PARTHIA: THE ROMAN WEST AND THE
PARTHIAN EAST
By J. B. Ward-Perkins **51**, 175
PASCAL, BLAISE (MM)
By H. F. STEWART **28**, 197
PAST AND FUTURE IN SHAKESPEARE'S
DRAMA (S)
By W. Clemen **52**, 231
PASTONS: THE LANGUAGE OF THE (IG)
By N. Davis **40**, 119
PATERNITY IN SHAKESPEARE (S)
By Sir A. Quiller-Couch **18**, 93
PATRIOTISM IN THE POETRY OF THE
EARLY EIGHTEENTH CENTURY
(W)
By B. Dobrée **35**, 49

PECOCK, REYNOLD, BISHOP OF CHI-
CHESTER (R)
By E. F. Jacob 37, 121
PELAGIUS
The Commentary of Pelagius on
the Epistle of St. Paul. By A.
Souter 2, 409
The Character and History of
Pelagius' Commentary. By A.
Souter 7, 261
PENINSULAR WAR, COLUMN AND LINE
IN THE
By Sir C. W. C. Oman 4, 321
PERFORMANCE OF CHRISTOPHER
MARLOWE's DR FAUSTUS, THE (C)
By N. Alexander 57, 331
PERSIAN CONSTITUTIONAL MOVEMENT,
THE
By E. G. Browne 8, 311
PERSIAN TRANSLITERATION
Report of committee 8, 505
PERSON AND OFFICE IN SHAKESPEARE's
PLAYS (S)
By P. Edwards 56, 93
PERSONAL ROLE OF SIMON DE MONT-
FORT IN THE PERIOD OF BARONIAL
REFORM AND REBELLION, THE,
1258–65 (R)
By R. F. Treharne 40, 75
PETRUS PEREGRINUS DE MARICOURT
AND HIS EPISTOLA DE MAGNETE
By S. P. Thompson 2, 377
PHAROS OF ALEXANDRIA, THE
By Don Miguel de Asin 19, 277
PHENOMENALISM (P)
By J. L. Mackie 55, 113
PHILOSOPHICAL OPINION IN AMERICA
(P)
By G. Santayana 8, 299
PHILOSOPHY OF ANALYSIS, THE (P)
By B. Blandshard 38, 39
PHILOSOPHY OF HISTORY, THE (P)
By A. S. Pringle-Pattison 10, 513
Some Problems of the Philosophy of
History (P). By G. C. Field
24, 55
PHILOSOPHY OF LANGUAGE IN REVOLU-
TIONARY FRANCE, THE (DH)
By H. B. Acton 45, 199

PHONETICS
The Study of English Speech by
new Methods of Phonetic Investi-
gation. By E. W. Scripture
10, 271
PICTOGRAPHIC AND LINEAR SCRIPTS
OF MINÔAN CRETE AND THEIR
RELATIONS, THE
By Sir A. J. Evans 1, 137
PLACE OF HENRY I IN ENGLISH
HISTORY, THE (R)
By R. W. Southern 48, 127
PLACE-NAMES
English Place-name Study. By Sir
A. Mawer 10, 31
Place-names and the Anglo-Saxon
Settlement (IG). By A. H. Smith
42, 67
The Significance of English Place-
names (IG). By K. Cameron
62, 135
PLATO AND THE AUTHORSHIP OF THE
'EPINOMIS'
By A. E. Taylor 15, 235
PLATONISM OF ARISTOTLE, THE (DH)
By G. E. L. Owen 51, 125
PLATO's BIOGRAPHY OF SOCRATES
By A. E. Taylor 8, 93
PLATO's REPUBLIC, MENTAL HEALTH
IN (DH)
By A. J. P. Kenny 55, 229
PLEA FOR THE LIBERTY OF INTER-
PRETING, A (S)
By L. Abercrombie 16, 137
PLOTINUS (MM)
By the Very Revd. W. R. Inge
15, 19
POEMS OF LLYWARCH HÊN, THE
(JR)
By I. Williams 18, 269
POETIC ROMANCERS AFTER 1850 (W)
By O. Elton 6, 413
POETRY
On the History of the Ballads, 1100–
1500. By W. P. Ker 4, 179
The Historical Character of English
Lyric (W). By G. Saintsbury
5, 475

POETRY (*cont.*):

The Connexion between Ancient and Modern Romance (W). By W. J. Courthope   5, 245

The Influence of English Poetry upon the Romantic Revival on the Continent (W). By C. Vaughan   6, 261

Poetic Romancers after 1850 (W) By O. Elton   6, 413

Is there a Poetic View of the World? (W). By C. H. Herford   7, 423

The Revelation of England through her Poetry (W). By H. Walker   8, 181

English Poetry in its Relation to Painting and the other Arts (AC). By L. Binyon   8, 381

Poetry and Time (W). By Sir H. Newbolt   8, 487

Some Recent Studies in English Prosody. By G. Saintsbury   9, 79

Poetry and Commonplace (W). By J. Bailey   9, 213

Some Contributions to the English Anthology (W). By J. Drinkwater   10, 181

The Criticism of Poetry (W). By F. L. Lucas   19, 167

Poetry in Prose (W). By W. de la Mare   21, 239

The English Epic Tradition (W). By E. M. W. Tillyard   22, 35

The Poet and the Past (W). By Edith C. Batho   23, 29

Romantic Poetry and the Fine Arts (W). By E. Blunden   28, 101

The Manner of Proceeding in certain Eighteenth- and early Nineteenth-century Poems (W). By G. Tillotson   34, 139

Patriotism in the Poetry of the early Eighteenth Century (W). By B. Dobrée   35, 49

Changing Views of the Mind in English Poetry (W). By G. Bullough   41, 61

Poetry and Interpretation (W). By Joan Bennett   44, 185

Lapidary Verse (W). By R. W. Ketton-Cremer   45, 237

Great Poetry (W). By J. H. A. Sparrow   46, 217

The Study of Form and the Renewal of Poetry (W). By F. T. Prince   50, 45

The Common Privileges of Poetry (W). By Winifred Nowottny   52, 61

Medieval Poetry and the Figural View of Reality (IG). By Elizabeth Salter   54, 73

The Poetic Powers of Repetition (W). By Kathleen Lea   55, 51

The Nature of Alliterative Poetry in Late Medieval England (IG). By G. Shepherd   56, 57

Waste Land, Holy Land (W). By Kathleen Raine   62, 379

Provenance and Problematics of 'Sublime and Alarming Images' in Poetry (W). By E. Morgan   63, 293

POETRY OF LORD BYRON, THE (W) By J. Buxton   56, 77

POETRY OF CÆDMON, THE (IG) By C. L. Wrenn   32, 277

POETRY OF COLLINS, THE (W) By H. W. Garrod   14, 21

POETRY OF WILLIAM COLLINS, THE (W) By A. Johnston   59, 321

POETRY OF THE EARLY WAVERLEY NOVELS, THE (C) By Clare Lamont   61, 315

POETRY OF UGOLO FOSCOLO, THE (I) By A. Cippico   11, 13

POETRY OF THOMAS GRAY, THE (W) By Lord David Cecil   31, 43

POETRY OF THOMAS GRAY, THE: VERSIONS OF THE SELF (C) By R. Lonsdale   59, 105

POETRY OF SIR WALTER SCOTT, THE (C) By D. Davie   47, 61

POETS AND THEIR CRITICS: LANGLAND
AND MILTON (W)
By R. W. Chambers 27, 109
POLITICAL ECONOMY OF INFLATION,
THE (K)
By T. Wilson 61, 291
POLITICAL SIGNIFICANCE OF 'GULLI-
VER'S TRAVELS', THE
By Sir C. H. Firth 9, 237
POLITICS IN THE FIRST WORLD WAR
(R)
By A. J. P. Taylor 45, 67
POMPEII: ON THE DIONYSIAC FRESCO
IN THE VILLA DEI MISTERI
By G. Zuntz 49, 177
POPE
Wordsworth and Pope (W). By J.
R. Sutherland 30, 33
POPE AND DULNESS (C)
By Emrys Jones 54, 231
POPE'S POETICAL MANUSCRIPTS (W)
By J. Butt 40, 23
PORSON, RICHARD (1759–1808)
By Sir D. Page 45, 221
PORTRAIT OF THE ARTIST AS PROTEUS,
A (S)
By M. Grivelet 61, 153
PORTRAITS
The English Historical Portrait:
Document and Myth (AA). By
H. M. Hake 29, 133
The British School of Miniature
Portrait-painters (AA). By C.
Winter 34, 119
The Development of the British
Literary Portrait up to Samuel
Johnson (AA). By D. Piper (AA)
54, 51
PORTUGUESE EMPIRE, THE COLOUR
QUESTION, 1415–1825 (R)
By C. R. Boxer 47, 113
POSITION OF AN ACADEMY IN A CIVI-
LISED STATE, THE
Presidential Address. By Sir F. G.
Kenyon 8, 37
POSITION LINGUISTIQUE DU CELTIQUE,
LA (JR)
By J. Vendryes 23, 333

POTTER AND PAINTER IN ANCIENT
ATHENS
By Sir J. D. Beazley 30, 87
PREDICTING AND DECIDING (P)
By D. Pears 50, 193
PRE-ESTABLISHED HARMONY VERSUS
CONSTANT CONJUNCTION: THE DIS-
TINCTION BETWEEN RATIONALISM
AND EMPIRICISM (DH)
By H. Ishiguro 63, 239
PRESENT STATE OF MEDIAEVAL STUDIES
IN GREAT BRITAIN, THE
By T. F. Tout 6, 151
PRESIDENTIAL ADDRESSES
By Lord Reay on 26 June 1903 1, 1
By Lord Reay on 29 June 1904
1, 17
By Lord Reay on 5 July 1905 2, 1
By Lord Reay on 28 June 1906
2, 7
By Lord Reay on 11 June 1907
3, 1
By Sir E. M. Thompson on 25 June
1908 3, 7
By Sir E. M. Thompson on 1 July
1909 4, 1
By S. H. Butcher, on 28 June 1910
4, 9
On 'Tennyson' by S. H. Butcher
4, 21
By Lord Reay (acting president) on
5 July 1911 5, 3
By Sir A. W. Ward on 25 October
1911 5, 15
By Sir A. W. Ward on 1 July 1912
5, 7
By Sir A. W. Ward on 30 October
1912 5, 23
By Sir A. W. Ward on 1 July 1913
6, 1
By Viscount Bryce on 10 July 1914
6, 7
At the International Congress of
Historical Studies 1913. By Viscount Bryce and Sir A. W. Ward
6, 113
By Viscount Bryce on 30 June 1915
7, 1

PRESIDENTIAL ADDRESSES (*cont.*):

By Viscount Bryce on 14 July 1916
7, 17

The Next Thirty Years. By Viscount Bryce on 19 July 1917 **8**, 1

The Position of an Academy in a Civilised State. By Sir F. G. Kenyon on 4 July 1918 **8**, 37

By Sir F. G. Kenyon on 3 July 1919
9, 1

International Scholarship. By Sir F. G. Kenyon on 21 July 1920
9, 21

The Fellowship of Learning. By Sir F. G. Kenyon on 6 July 1921
10, 3

By H. A. L. Fisher on 13 July 1932
18, 15

By J. W. Mackail on 12 July 1933
19, 19

By J. W. Mackail on 11 July 1934
20, 17

By J. W. Mackail on 10 July 1935
21, 19

By J. W. Mackail, 1936 **22**, 21

By Sir W. D. Ross on 14 July 1937
23, 21

By Sir W. D. Ross, July 1938
24, 21

By Sir W. D. Ross on 12 July 1939
25, 23

By Sir W. D. Ross on 10 July 1940
26, 19

By Sir J. H. Clapham on 9 July 1941
27, 19

By Sir J. H. Clapham on 15 July 1942 **28**, 13

By Sir J. H. Clapham on 14 July 1943 **29**, 13

By Sir J. H. Clapham on 12 July 1944 **30**, 13

By Sir J. H. Clapham on 11 July 1945 **31**, 13

By Sir H. I. Bell on 16 July 1947
33, 19

By Sir H. I. Bell on 14 July 1948
34, 15

By Sir H. I. Bell on 13 July 1949
35, 15

By Sir H. I. Bell on 12 July 1950
36, 15

By Sir C. K. Webster on 11 July 1951 **37**, 15

By Sir C. K. Webster on 6 June 1952 **38**, 13

By Sir C. K. Webster on 8 July 1953
39, 15

By Sir C. K. Webster on 7 July 1954
40, 15

By Sir G. N. Clark on 6 July 1955
41, 15

By Sir G. N. Clark on 4 July 1956
42, 17

By Sir G. N. Clark on 10 July 1957
43, 17

By Sir G. N. Clark on 9 July 1958
44, 15

By Sir C. M. Bowra on 8 July 1959
45, 17

By Sir C. M. Bowra on 6 July 1960
46, 29

By Sir C. M. Bowra on 5 July 1961
47, 27

By Sir C. M. Bowra on 11 July 1962
48, 31

By Lord Robbins on 10 July 1963
49, 43

By Lord Robbins on 8 July 1964
50, 37

By Lord Robbins on 7 July 1965
51, 39

By Lord Robbins ('Comments') on 6 July 1966 **52**, 41

By Lord Robbins on 12 July 1967
53, 39

By Sir K. C. Wheare on 10 July 1968 **54**, 45

By Sir K. C. Wheare on 9 July 1969
55, 45

By Sir K. C. Wheare on 8 July 1970
56, 51

By Sir K. C. Wheare on 7 July 1971
57, 59

By Sir D. Page on 12 July 1972
58, 61

By Sir D. Page on 11 July 1973
59, 57

By Sir D. Page on 10 July 1974
60, 129

By Sir I. Berlin on 10 July 1975
61, 71

By Sir I. Berlin on 1 July 1976
62, 85

By Sir I. Berlin on 30 June 1977
63, 1

PRESUPPOSITIONS AND FINITE TRUTHS (P)
By Dorothy Emmet 35, 67

PRIMACY OF PRACTICAL REASON, THE (DH)
By G. J. Warnock 52, 253

PRIMITIVE MAN
By G. Eliot Smith 7, 455

PRINCIPLES OF EMENDATION IN SHAKE-SPEARE (S)
By Sir W. W. Greg 14, 147

PRINTERS AND READERS IN ITALY IN THE FIFTEENTH CENTURY (I)
By V. Scholderer 35, 25

PRINTING, THE ART OF (AA)
By S. Morison 23, 373

PRIVACY (P)
By Sir A. J. Ayer 45, 43

PROBABILITY—THE ONE AND THE MANY (P)
By L. J. Cohen 61, 83

PROBLEM OF SPELLING REFORM, THE
By Revd. W. W. Skeat 2, 247

PROBLEMS AND ROLES OF THE AMERICAN ARTIST AS PORTRAYED BY THE AMERICAN NOVELIST (STP)
By P. A. Tanner 57, 159

PROLEGOMENA TO THE STUDY OF THE LATER IRISH BARDS, 1200–1500
By E. C. Quiggin 5, 89

PROOF OF AN EXTERNAL WORLD (P)
By G. E. Moore 25, 273

PROPOSED CHANGES IN NAVAL PRIZE LAW
By Sir T. E. Holland 5, 144

PROSODY, SOME RECENT STUDIES IN ENGLISH
By G. Saintsbury 9, 79

PROVENANCE AND PROBLEMATICS OF 'SUBLIME AND ALARMING IMAGES' IN POETRY (W)
By E. Morgan 63, 293

PSALMS, THE: A NEW FRAGMENT
By J. W. B. Barns and G. D. Kilpatrick 43, 229

PSYCHOLOGICAL ELEMENTS IN GREEK SCULPTURE
By P. Gardner 1, 251

PUZZLING ELEMENT IN THE NOTION OF THINKING, A (P)
By G. Ryle 44, 129

Q

QUALITY OF LIFE, THE (P)
By Sir W. Mitchell 20, 249

QUARRYING IN ANTIQUITY (MW)
By J. B. Ward-Perkins 57, 137

R

RALEIGH'S HISTORY OF THE WORLD
By Sir C. H. Firth 8, 427

RANALLI, FERDINANDO: A LONELY PATRIOT (I)
By Sir W. K. Hancock 27, 275

RANDOLPH, THOMAS (W)
By G. C. Moore Smith 13, 79

READING SHAKESPEARE, ON (S)
By M. R. Ridley 26, 197

REALISM, THE BASIS OF
By S. Alexander 6, 279

REASON AND INTUITION (P)
By A. C. Ewing 27, 67

RECENTI CONTROVERSIE INTORNO ALL' UNITÀ DELLA STORIA D'ITALIA (I)
By B. Croce 22, 57

RECORDS OF THE VENETIC LANGUAGE, THE
By R. S. Conway 3, 159

REFORM BY STATUTE: THOMAS STARKEY'S DIALOGUE AND THOMAS CROMWELL'S POLICY (R)
By G. R. Elton 54, 165

RELATIONS BETWEEN SPOKEN AND WRITTEN LANGUAGE, ON THE
By H. BRADLEY   6, 211

RELATIONS OF THE HOUSE OF SAVOY WITH THE COURT OF ENGLAND, THE
By Sir F. de Filippi   8, 447

RELATIONS OF MORALITY TO RELIGION, THE (P)
By W. G. de Burgh   21, 75

RENAISSANCE OF ARCHITECTURE AND STONE-CARVING IN SOUTHERN FRANCE IN THE TENTH AND ELEVENTH CENTURIES, THE (AA)
By Sir A. W. Clapham   18, 47

REPORT OF DISCOVERIES OF ROMAN REMAINS IN BRITAIN IN 1912
By F. J. Haverfield   5, 409

RE-READING THE DIVINE COMEDY (I)
By E. R. Vincent   31, 223

RE-READING KEYNES, ON (K)
By Lord Kahn   60, 361

REVELATION XX-4–XXII: THE ORIGINAL ORDER OF THE TEXT
By the Ven. C. H. Charles   7, 37

REVELATION OF ENGLAND THROUGH HER POETRY, THE (W)
By H. Walker   8, 181

RHŶS, SIR JOHN (JR)
By Sir J. Morris-Jones   11, 187

'RIGHTEOUSNESS' IN THE GOSPELS
By Revd. E. A. Abbott   8, 351

RIGHTS OF NEUTRALS, THE
By Sir E. Fry   2, 265

RISE OF NORMANDY, THE (R)
By D. Douglas   33, 101

ROCHESTER, JOHN WILMOT, EARL OF (C)
By Anne Righter   53, 47

ROLE OF BOSNIA IN INTERNATIONAL POLITICS, THE (1875–1914) (R)
By R. W. Seton-Watson   17, 335

ROLE AND CHARACTER OF THE CIVIL SERVICE, THE (TOB)
By Sir W. Armstrong   56, 209

ROMAN BRITAIN
The Romanisation of Roman Britain. By F. J. Haverfield   2, 185

First Report on Recent Excavations in Roman Britain. By F. J. Haverfield   4, 319

Report of Discoveries of Roman Remains in Britain in 1912. By F. J. Haverfield   5, 409

Roman Britain and Roman Military Antiquities (AR). By Sir I. A. Richmond   41, 297

Britain and Julius Caesar (MW). By C. F. C. Hawkes   63, 125

ROMAN NUMISMATICS: MISCELLANEOUS NOTES
By H. Mattingly   43, 179

Further Miscellaneous Notes. By H. Mattingly   46, 249

ROMAN WEST AND THE PARTHIAN EAST, THE
By J. B. Ward-Perkins   51, 175

ROMANCE, THE CONNECTION BETWEEN ANCIENT AND MODERN
By W. J. Courthope   5, 245

ROMANESQUE RELIEF IN YORK MINSTER, A
By Sir E. Maclagan   10, 479

ROMANISATION OF ROMAN BRITAIN, THE
By F. J. Haverfield   2, 185

ROMANS
Who were the Romans? By Sir W. Ridgeway   3, 17

The Virtues of a Roman Emperor (R). By Revd. M. P. Charlesworth   23, 105

ROMANTIC POETRY AND THE FINE ARTS (W)
By E. Blunden   28, 101

ROMANTICISM AND REGIONALISM (I)
By C. Pellizzi   15, 135

ROME BEYOND THE SOUTHERN EGYPTIAN FRONTIER (MW)
By L. P. Kirwan   63, 13

'ROMEO AND JULIET' AS AN EXPERIMENTAL TRAGEDY (S)
By H. B. Charlton   25, 143

ROSE OF THE WINDS, THE
By S. P. Thompson   6, 179

ROSES, THE WARS OF THE (R)
By K. B. McFarlane   50, 87

ROSTOVTZEFF'S *IRANIANS AND GREEKS*
By D. G. Hogarth 10, 356
ROUSSEAU (MM)
By J. Starobinski 62, 95
RULES, PERCEPTION AND INTELLIGI-
BILITY
By F. A. Hayek 48, 321
RUSKIN (MM)
By R. W. Livingstone 31, 85
RUSSELL, BERTRAND, as a Philosopher
(MM)
By Sir A. J. Ayer 58, 127
RUSSIA: EARLY MAN IN THE SOVIET
UNION (AR)
By C. B. M. McBurney 61, 171
RUSSIAN REVOLUTION AND THE
PEASANT, THE (R)
By E. H. Carr 49, 69

S

SAGA AND THE MYTH OF SIR THOMAS
MORE, THE (LH)
By R. W. Chambers 12, 179
ST. PAUL, THE MIND OF (MM)
By T. R. Glover 27, 247
SAINT THOMAS AQUINAS (MM)
By E. Gilson 21, 29
SAINTS' LIVES: THE EARLIEST WRITTEN
IN ENGLAND (IG)
By B. Colgrave 44, 35
SALISBURY, JOHN OF: THE EARLY
CORRESPONDENCE OF
By R. L. Poole 11, 27
SAMSON AGONISTES AND THE HELLENIC
DRAMA
By Sir R. C. Jebb 3, 341
SAVOY, THE HOUSE OF, RELATIONS
WITH THE COURT OF ENGLAND
By Sir F. de Filippi 8, 447
SCEPTICAL ANTHROPOLOGIST, THE?
SOCIAL ANTHROPOLOGY AND
MARXIST VIEWS ON SOCIETY (RB)
By Sir R. W. Firth 58, 177
SCHLIEMANN'S TROY—ONE HUNDRED
YEARS AFTER (MW)
By M. I. Finley 60, 393

SCOTT, ALEXANDER, AND SCOTTISH
COURT POETRY OF THE MIDDLE
SIXTEENTH-CENTURY (W)
By J. Macqueen 54, 93
SCOTT, THE POETRY OF THE EARLY
WAVERLEY NOVELS (C)
By Clare Lamont 61, 315
SCOTT, SIR WALTER, THE POETRY OF
(C)
By D. Davie 47, 61
SCOTTISH ALLITERATIVE POEMS, THE
(IG)
By Sir W. A. Craigie 28, 217
SCULPTURE
Psychological Elements in Greek
Sculpture. By P. Gardner 1, 251
Trajan's Column. By G. Boni
3, 93
A Romanesque Relief in York
Minster. By Sir E. Maclagan
10, 479
The Appreciation of Sculpture
(AA). By Sir E. Maclagan
11, 311
Late Archaic and Early Classical
Greek Sculpture in Sicily and
South Italy (AA). By B. Ashmole
20, 91
The Western Aspects of Gandhara
Sculpture. By H. Buchtal
31, 151
The Ara Pacis Reconsidered (I). By
J. M. C. Toynbee 39, 67
Some Nameless Sculptors of the
Fifth Century BC (AA). By B.
Ashmole 48, 213
Inigo Jones (MM). By Sir J.
Summerson 50, 169
1066 and Architectural Sculpture
(AA). By G. Zarnecki 52, 87
The Dancing Siva in Early South
Indian Art (MW). By D. Barrett
62, 181
SCYTHIANS
The Art of the Northern Nomads
(AA). By Sir E. H. Minns 28, 47
SEALS AND DOCUMENTS
By R. L. Poole 9, 319

SEALS OF ANCIENT INDIAN STYLE, FOUND AT UR
By C. J. Gadd   18, 191

SELEUCID-PARTHIAN STUDIES
By Sir W. W. Tarn   16, 105

SENATORS IN THE EMPEROR'S SERVICE
By E. Birley   39, 197

SENTENCE IN WELSH, THE (JR)
By H. Lewis   28, 259

SHAKESPEARE

Shakesperiana, 1598–1602. By Sir I. Gollancz   1, 199

'What to expect of Shakespeare' (S). By J. J. Jusserand   5, 223

Coriolanus (S). By A. C. Bradley   5, 457

Shakespeare and Germany (S). By A. Brandl   6, 249

Hamlet and Orestes (S). By G. Murray   6, 389

Shakespeare and the Italian Renaissance (S). By Sir S. Lee   7, 121

Cervantes and Shakespeare (MM). By J. Fitzmaurice-Kelly   7, 297

Shakespeare after Three Hundred Years (S). By J. W. Mackail   7, 319

The Character of Shakespeare (S). By the Very Revd. H. C. Beeching   8, 157

Shakespeare and England (S). By Sir W. Raleigh   8, 403

Shakespeare and the Makers of Virginia (S). By Sir A. W. Ward   9, 141

The Foundation of Shakespeare's Text (S). By A. W. Pollard   10, 379

The Disintegration of Shakespeare (S). By Sir E. K. Chambers   11, 89

From Henry V to Hamlet (S). By H. Granville-Barker   11, 283

The Bacchic Element in Shakespeare's Plays (S). By E. Legouis   12, 115

Shakespeare in America (S). By A. Thorndike   13, 153

Principles of Emendation in Shakespeare (S). By Sir W. W. Greg   14, 147

The Elizabethan Shakespeare (S). By J. Dover Wilson   15, 101

A Plea for the Liberty of Interpreting (S). By L. Abercrombie   16, 137

Shakespeare's Iterative Imagery (S). By Caroline F. E. Spurgeon   17, 147

Paternity in Shakespeare (S). By Sir A. Quiller-Couch   18, 93

The Treatment of Shakespeare's Text by his Earlier Editors, 1709–1768 (S). By R. B. McKerrow   19, 89

The Mythical Sorrows of Shakespeare (S). By C. J. Sisson   20, 45

The Theme of Revenge in Elizabethan Tragedy (S). By P. Simpson   21, 101

Style in Shakespeare (S). By O. Elton   22, 69

The Jacobean Shakespeare and Measure for Measure (S). By R. W. Chambers   23, 135

The Baroque Character of the Elizabethan Tragic Hero (S). By L. L. Schücking   24, 85

'Romeo and Juliet' as an Experimental Tragedy (S). By H. B. Charlton   25, 143

On Reading Shakespeare (S). By M. R. Ridley   26, 197

Shakespeare and the Diction of Common Life (S). By F. P. Wilson   27, 167

Hamlet: the Prince or the Poem? (S) By C. S. Lewis   28, 139

Aspects of Classical Legend and History in Shakespeare (S). By F. S. Boas   29, 107

Shakespeare's Audience (S). By H. S. Bennett   30, 73

Shakespeare's Punctuation (S). By P. Alexander   31, 61

The Golden World of 'King Lear' (S). By G. L. Bickersteth   32, 147

Shakespeare and the Termers (S).
By G. M. Young   33, 81
Shakespeare the Dramatist (S). By
Una Ellis-Fermor   34, 81
Shakespeare in Spain (S). By Sir H.
Thomas   35, 87
The Emergence of Shakespeare's
Tragedy (S). By H. V. D. Dyson
36, 69
Shakespeare's Poetic Energy (S).
By G. Rylands   37, 99
Co-operation in Shakespearian
Scholarship (S). By Allardyce
Nicoll   38, 71
Shakespeare's Earliest Years in the
Theatre (S). By J. Isaacs 39, 119
Language and Poetry in Shake-
speare's Early Plays (S). By Gladys
D. Willcock   40, 103
The Noble Moor (S). By Dame
Helen L. Gardner   41, 189
Shakespeare's Politics, and the
Nature of Tradition (S). By L. C.
Knights   43, 115
Shakespeare and the Tragic Pattern
(S). By K. Muir   44, 145
The Tyranny of Shakespeare (S).
By T. J. B. Spencer   45, 153
Edward Capell and his Edition of
Shakespeare (S). By Alice Walker
46, 131
Shakespeare and the Players (S).
By R. David   47, 139
Shakespeare's Comic Insight (S).
By Mary Lascelles   48, 171
Hamlet and Ophelia (S). By Harold
Jenkins   49, 135
Shakespeare the Elizabethan (S).
By G. Bullough   50, 121
Shakespeare's Primitive Art (S). By
M. C. Bradbrook   51, 215
Past and Future in Shakespeare's
Drama (S). By W. Clemen
52, 231
Othello and Colour Prejudice (S).
By G. K. Hunter   53, 139
Shakespeare's Histories and 'The
Emotion of Multitude' (S). By
A. R. Humphreys   54, 265

Shakespeare without Words (S). By
A. Harbage   55, 129
Person and Office in Shakespeare's
Plays (S). By P. Edwards 56, 93
Shakespeare's Lofty Scene (S). By
J. I. M. Stewart   57, 181
Unblotted Lines: Shakespeare at
Work (S). By Molly M. Mahood
58, 163
Shakespeare's Tragic Fiction (S).
By C. Leech   59, 159
Measure for Measure: the Play and
the Themes (S). By J. C. Maxwell
60, 199
A Portrait of the Artist as Proteus
(S). By M. Grivelet   61, 153
'Upon Such Sacrifices' (S). By P.
Brockbank   62, 109
Shakespeare and Baroque Art (S).
By Nicholas Brooke   63, 53
SHELBURNE, LORD, AND THE FOUND-
ING OF BRITISH-AMERICAN GOOD-
WILL (R)
By C. W. Alvord   11, 369
SHELLEY AND THE OPPRESSORS OF
MANKIND (W)
By G. Gordon   10, 257
SHELLEY, THE THEOLOGY OF (W)
By A. M. D. Hughes   24, 191
SHUMER AND SHEM: SOME PHILOLOGI-
CAL COINCIDENCES AND SEQUENCES
By C. J. Ball   7, 85
SICILIAN NORMAN KINGDOM, THE, IN
THE MIND OF ANGLO-NORMAN
CONTEMPORARIES (I)
By Evelyn Jamison   24, 237
SIGNIFICANCE OF ENGLISH PLACE-
NAMES, THE (IG)
By K. Cameron   62, 135
SILVER COINAGE OF CRETE, THE
By Sir G. MacDonald   9, 289
SIMON DE MONTFORT'S ROLE, 1258–65
(R)
By R. F. Treharne   40, 75
SINCERITY AND INSINCERITY IN
CHARLES JAMES FOX (R)
By Sir H. Butterfield   57, 237
SIRIS, GEORGE BERKELEY'S (P)
By A. D. Ritchie   40, 41

SISTINE CHAPEL, THE: DECORATION OF (AA)
By J. Wild   44, 61
SKELTON (C)
By J. Holloway   44, 83
SLAVONIC TRANSLITERATION
Report of Committee   8, 523
SMITH, ADAM (MM)
By W. R. Scott   10, 435
Studies relating to Adam Smith during the last fifty years. By W. R. Scott   26, 249
SOCIAL ANTHROPOLOGY: A NATURAL SCIENCE OF SOCIETY? (RB)
By Sir E. Leach   62, 157
SOCRATIC DOCTRINE OF THE SOUL, THE (P)
By J. Burnet   7, 235
SOME ALEXANDRIAN FORGERIES
By P. M. Fraser   47, 243
SOME ASPECTS OF THE AMERICAN SHORT STORY (STP)
By W. E. Allen   59, 125
SOME ASPECTS OF ANCIENT ARABIC POETRY
By Sir C. J. Lyall   8, 365
SOME ASPECTS OF THE EGYPTIAN LANGUAGE
By Sir A. H. Gardiner   23, 81
SOME ASPECTS OF THE GENIUS OF GIOVANNI BOCCACCIO (I)
By E. Hutton   10, 219
SOME ASPECTS OF KIPLING'S VERSE (C)
By A. Rutherford   51, 375
SOME ATTIC VASES IN THE CYPRUS MUSEUM
By Sir J. D. Beazley   33, 195
SOME CARDINAL POINTS IN KNOWLEDGE
By S. H. Hodgson   5, 28
SOME CONDOTTIERI OF THE TRECENTO (I)
By D. M. Bueno de Mesquita   32, 219
SOME CONSIDERATIONS ON THE PRESENT STATE OF HISTORICAL STUDIES (R)
By E. L. Woodward   36, 95

SOME CONTRIBUTIONS TO THE ENGLISH ANTHOLOGY (W)
By J. Drinkwater   10, 181
SOME ELEMENTS IN HEGEL'S LOGIC (DH)
By G. R. G. Mure   44, 21
SOME FRESH DOCUMENTS CONCERNING THE ITALIAN RISORGIMENTO BEFORE 1849 (I)
By G. F-H. Berkeley   26, 227
SOME NAMELESS SCULPTORS OF THE FIFTH CENTURY BC (AA)
By B. Ashmole   48, 213
SOME NEW STUDIES OF THE ROMAN REPUBLICAN COINAGE
By H. Mattingly   39, 239
SOME PALESTINIAN CULTS IN THE GRAECO-ROMAN AGE
By Sir G. F. Hill   5, 411
SOME PROBLEMS IN MEDIEVAL HISTORIOGRAPHY (R)
By G. G. Coulton   18, 155
SOME PROBLEMS OF THE PHILOSOPHY OF HISTORY (P)
By G. C. Field   24, 55
SOME PROBLEMS OF SELF-REFERENCE IN JOHN BURIDAN (DH)
By A. N. Prior   48, 281
SOME PROBLEMS ABOUT TIME (P)
By P. T. Geach   51, 321
SOME RECENT STUDIES IN ENGLISH PROSODY
By G. Saintsbury   9, 79
SOME RECENTLY DISCOVERED FRANCISCAN DOCUMENTS
By A. G. Little   12, 147
SOME REFLECTIONS ON CHAUCER'S 'ART POETICAL' (IG)
By Dorothy Everett   36, 131
SOME REFLECTIONS OF A MEDIEVAL CRIMINOLOGIST (R)
By R. B. Pugh   59, 83
SOME RESULTS OF RESEARCH IN THE HISTORY OF EDUCATION IN ENGLAND
By A. F. Leach   6, 433
SOME THEMES AND VARIATIONS IN THE POETRY OF ANDREW MARVELL (W)
By J. B. Leishman   47, 223

Some Uses and Misuses of the Terms Baroque and Rococo as applied to Architecture (AA)
By A. Blunt 58, 215

Song of Carlaverock and the Parliamentary Roll of Arms, The
By N. Denholm-Young 47, 251

Sophocles and the Perfect Number
By H. St. J. Thackeray 16, 15

Sound of American Literature a Century ago, The (STP)
By C. Bode 47, 97

Sources of Knowledge and of Ignorance, On the (P)
By Sir K. R. Popper 46, 39

South Africa: Lord Milner and (R)
By E. A. Walker 28, 155

South American Independence, British Merchants and (R)
By R. A. Humphreys 51, 151

Spelling Reform
The Problem of Spelling Reform.
By Revd. W. W. Skeat 2, 247

Spelman, Sir Henry, and the Concilia (R)
By Sir F. M. Powicke 16, 345

Spenser and the Allegorists (W)
By J. F. Kermode 48, 261

Spenseriana
By Sir I. Gollancz 3, 99

Spinoza (MM)
By W. R. Sorley 8, 469

Spinoza and the Idea of Freedom (DH)
By S. Hampshire 46, 195

Starkey's, Thomas, Dialogue and Thomas Cromwell's Policy (R)
By G. R. Elton 54, 165

Structure of the Kingdom of Ends, The (P)
By J. N. Findlay 43, 97

Structure of Stichomythia in Attic Tragedy, The
By Sir J. L. Myres 34, 199

Studies in Early Irish History
By Sir J. Rhŷs 1, 21

Studies relating to Adam Smith during the last Fifty Years
By W. R. Scott 26, 249

Study of Early Municipal History in England, The
By J. Tait 10, 201

Study of English Speech by New Methods of Phonetic Investigation, The
By E. W. Scripture 10, 271

Study of Form and the Renewal of Poetry, The (W)
By F. T. Prince 50, 45

Study of Manx Gaelic, The (JR)
By R. L. Thomson 55, 177

Study of Modern History in Great Britain, The
By Sir C. H. Firth 6, 139

Style in Shakespeare (S)
By O. Elton 22, 69

Suisse, La: Comment se Forme une Nation
By G. de Reynold 8, 427

Sultantepe, The Assyrian Tablets from
By O. R. Gurney 41, 21

Surkh Kotal, The Excavations at (AR)
By D. Schlumberger 47, 77

Survey of Research on an Early Phase of Celtic Culture, A (JR)
By J. M. de Navarro 22, 297

Survival of Anglo-Saxon Illumination After the Norman Conquest (AA)
By F. Wormald 30, 127

Swift, Jonathan (MM)
By I. Ehrenpreis 54, 149

Syriac
The Early Syriac Lectionary System.
By F. C. Burkitt 10, 301

Syriac Forms of New Testament Proper Names
By F. C. Burkitt 5, 377

T

TANGLED SKEIN, THE, ART IN ENGLAND 1800–1920 (AA)
By Sir R. Blomfield **9**, 375

TELEOLOGY
The Meaning of Teleology. By B. Bosanquet **2**, 235

1066 AND ARCHITECTURAL SCULPTURE (AA)
By G. Zarnecki **52**, 87

TENNYSON
Presidential Address. By S. H. Butcher **4**, 21
Tennyson. By Sir H. Jones **4**, 131
The Age of Tennyson (W). By G. M. Young **25**, 125

TENNYSON, WORDSWORTH AND (W)
By D. G. James **36**, 113

TENNYSON'S METHODS OF COMPOSITION (C)
By C. Ricks **52**, 209

TEPE YAHYA, EXCAVATIONS AT, 1967–1973 (AR)
By C. C. Lamberg-Karlovsky **59**, 283

TERCENTENARY OF THE BIRTH OF JOHN MILTON
By Sir A. W. Ward **3**, 213

TERCENTENARY OF MILTON'S BIRTH, THE
Lines by G. Meredith **3**, 353

TEXT OF ABBO OF FLEURY'S *QUAESTIONES GRAMMATICALES*, ON THE
By H. Bradley **10**, 173

THEME OF PATRIOTISM IN THE POETRY OF THE EARLY EIGHTEENTH CENTURY, THE (W)
By B. Dobrée **35**, 49

THEME OF REVENGE IN ELIZABETHAN TRAGEDY, THE (S)
By P. Simpson **21**, 101

THEOGNIS
By T. W. Allen **20**, 71

THEOLOGY OF SHELLEY, THE (W)
By A. M. D. Hughes **24**, 191

THERA, LIFE AND ART IN PREHISTORIC (AR)
By Sp. Marinatos **57**, 351

THINGS AND SENSATIONS
By G. F. Stout **2**, 169

THINKING AND REPRESENTATION (P)
By H. H. Price **32**, 83

THUCYDIDES (MM)
By Sir R. Syme **48**, 39

TIBERIUS AND PONTIUS PILATE IN ETHIOPIAN TRADITION AND POETRY
By E. Cerulli **59**, 141

TIME AND CHOICE (K)
By G. L. S. Shackle **62**, 309

'TIME' AND 'HISTORY' IN CONTEMPORARY PHILOSOPHY
By H. W. Carr **8**, 331

TIMES, BEGINNINGS AND CAUSES (P)
By G. E. M. Anscombe (Mrs Geach) **60**, 253

TOWARDS A CHAUCERIAN POETIC (IG)
By D. Brewer **60**, 219

TRADE UNION AND THE COMMON WEAL, THE (TOB)
By Sir H. Phelps Brown **53**, 165

TRAJAN'S COLUMN
By G. Boni **3**, 93

TRANSLITERATION OF ARABIC AND PERSIAN
Report of Committee **8**, 505

TRANSLITERATION OF SLAVONIC
Report of Committee **8**, 523

TREASURE-TROVE—THE LAW AND PRACTICE OF ANTIQUITY
By Sir G. F. Hill **19**, 219

TREATMENT OF SHAKESPEARE'S TEXT BY HIS EARLIER EDITORS, THE, 1709–1768 (S)
By R. B. McKerrow **19**, 89

TRIPOLITANIAN DISCOVERIES, AND THE ART OF THE SEVERAN AGE
By J. B. Ward Perkins **37**, 269

TROY, SCHLIEMANN'S—ONE HUNDRED YEARS AFTER (MW)
By M. I. Finley **60**, 393

TRUTH, INVENTION, AND THE MEANING OF LIFE (P)
By D. Wiggins **62**, 331

TSARDOM AND IMPERIALISM IN THE FAR EAST AND THE MIDDLE EAST, 1880–1914 (R)
By B. H. Sumner   27, 25

TWO BRANCHES OF THE SAME STREAM (Mac)
By E. N. Griswold   48, 235

TWO CELTIC WAVES IN SPAIN (JR)
By P. Bosch-Gimpera   26, 25

TWO PIONEERS OF ROMANTICISM; JOSEPH AND THOMAS WARTON (W)
By Sir E. Gosse   7, 145

TWO SOUTH ARABIAN INSCRIPTIONS
By D. S. Margoliouth   11, 177

TYRANNY OF SHAKESPEARE, THE (S)
By T. J. B. Spencer   45, 153

U

UNBLOTTED LINES: SHAKESPEARE AT WORK (S)
By Molly M. Mahood   58, 163

UNEXPLORED RELATIONSHIPS BETWEEN EARLY SEVENTEENTH-CENTURY VENETIAN OPERA AND CONTEMPORARY MUSIC IN FRANCE AND ENGLAND (I)
By R. Leppard   55, 99

UNIVERSALS AND PROPOSITIONS, THE NATURE OF (P)
By G. F. Stout   10, 157

UNRECOGNIZED WESTMINSTER CHRONICLER, AN 1381–1394
By the Very Revd. J. A. Robinson   3, 61

'UPON SUCH SACRIFICES' (S)
By P. Brockbank   62, 109

UR, SEALS OF ANCIENT INDIAN STYLE FOUND AT
By C. G. Gadd   18, 191

URBAN INTERACTION ON THE IRANIAN PLATEAU: EXCAVATIONS AT TEPE YAHYA, 1967–1973 (AR)
By C. C. Lamberg-Karlovsky   59, 283

USE OF DICTATION IN ANCIENT BOOK-PRODUCTION, THE
By T. C. Skeat   42, 179

UTHRED OF BOLDON, THE CENSURED OPINIONS OF
By Revd. M. D. Knowles   37, 305

V

VALUE AND THE METHODS OF MYTHOLOGIC STUDY, THE
By L. R. Farnell   9, 37

VARIOUS NUMISMATIC NOTES
By H. Mattingly   49, 313

VATICAN STANZE, THE: FUNCTIONS AND DECORATION (I)
By J. Shearman   57, 369

VENETIC LANGUAGE
The Records of the Venetic Language. By R. S. Conway   3, 159

VERGIL'S CREATIVE ART (AA)
By R. S. Conway   17, 17

VIOLENCE IN AMERICAN SOCIETY (STP)
By H. G. Nicholas   55, 145

VIRGIL IN ENGLISH POETRY (W)
By G. Gordon   17, 39

VIRGIL (MM)
By J. W. Mackail   17, 55

VIRGIL IN ITALIAN POETRY (I)
By E. G. Gardner   17, 75

VIRTUES OF A ROMAN EMPEROR, THE: PROPAGANDA AND THE CREATION OF BELIEF (R)
By Revd. M. P. Charlesworth   23, 105

W

WALES
Edward I's Castle-Building in Wales (JR). By Sir J. G. Edwards   32, 15

The Court Poets of the Welsh Princes (JR). By J. Lloyd-Jones   34, 167

The Normans and the Welsh March (R). By Sir J. G. Edwards   42, 155

WALES (*cont.*):
Castle-Building in Thirteenth-century Wales and Savoy (AR).
By A. J. Taylor   63, 265
WALES AND ARCHAEOLOGY (JR)
By Sir R. E. M. Wheeler   15, 319
WANDERING ENGLISHMEN IN ITALY (I)
By Mrs G. M. Trevelyan   16, 61
WANLEY, HUMPHREY: SAXONIST AND LIBRARY-KEEPER (IG)
By C. E. Wright   46, 99
WARS OF THE ROSES, THE (R)
By K. B. McFarlane   50, 87
WARTON, THOMAS (W)
By W. P. Ker   4, 349
WARTON, JOSEPH AND THOMAS: TWO PIONEERS OF ROMANTICISM (W).
By Sir E. Gosse   7, 145
WARTON'S HISTORY OF ENGLISH POETRY (W).
By D. Nichol Smith   15, 73
WARTON, THOMAS, AND THE EARLY POEMS OF MILTON (W)
By L. C. Martin   20, 25
WAS THE FAILURE OF THE SPANISH ARMADA DUE TO STORMS?
By J. H. Rose   22, 207
WASTE LAND, HOLY LAND (W)
By Kathleen Raine   62, 379
WELSH CHRONICLES, THE (JR)
By Sir J. E. Lloyd   14, 369
WELSH LATIN CHRONICLES, THE: AN-NALES CAMBRIÆ AND RELATED TEXTS (JR)
By Kathleen Hughes   59, 233
WELSH LITERARY RENASCENCE OF THE TWENTIETH CENTURY, THE (JR)
By Sir H. I. Bell   39, 139
WELSH METRICAL TREATISE, THE, ATTRIBUTED TO EINION OFFEIRIAD (JR)
By T. Parry   47, 177
WELSH POETIC DICTION (JR)
By J. H. Parry-Williams   32, 243
WELSH, THE SENTENCE IN (JR)
By H. Lewis   28, 259
WELSH? WHO ARE THE (JR)
By G. E. Daniel   40, 145

WESTERN ASPECTS OF GANDHARA SCULPTURE, THE (AA)
By H. Buchtal   31, 151
WESTERN TEXT IN THE GOSPELS AND ACTS, THE
By Sir F. G. Kenyon   24, 287
WESTMINSTER
An Unrecognised Westminster Chronicler 1381–1394. By the Very Revd. J. A. Robinson   3, 61
The Nave of Westminster. By Revd. R. B. Rackham   4, 33
Medieval Paintings at Westminster (AA). By W. R. Lethaby 13, 123
Paintings in Westminster Abbey, and contemporary Paintings (AA)
By F. Wormald   35, 161
'WHAT TO EXPECT OF SHAKESPEARE' (S)
By J. J. Jusserand   5, 223
WHAT'S REALLY WRONG WITH PHENOMENALISM? (P)
By J. L. Mackie   55, 113
WHIG HISTORIANS, THE (R)
By H. A. L. Fisher   14, 297
WHO WERE THE ROMANS?
By Sir W. Ridgeway   3, 17
WHO ARE THE WELSH? (JR)
By G. E. Daniel   40, 145
WILMOT, JOHN, EARL OF ROCHESTER (C)
By Anne Righter   53, 47
WINNING OF THE INITIATIVE BY THE HOUSE OF COMMONS, THE (R)
By W. Notestein   11, 125
WORDSWORTH, WILLIAM, 1770–1969 (C)
By J. Wordsworth   55, 211
WORDSWORTH AND POPE (W)
By J. R. Sutherland   30, 33
WORDSWORTH AND THE SEVENTEENTH CENTURY (W)
By J. Crofts   26, 179
WORDSWORTH AND TENNYSON (W)
By D. G. James   36, 113

WORDSWORTH'S EARLY POETRY: THE
    FIGURE IN A LANDSCAPE (W)
    By R. Sharrock   **58**, 313
WORLD HISTORY (R)
    By Viscount Bryce   **9**, 187
WULFSTAN'S PROSE (IG)
    By A. McIntosh   **35**, 109
WYCLIF, JOHN: THE PATH TO DISSENT
    (R)
    By G. Leff   **52**, 143

Y

YEATS, W. B.: POET AND CRANK (C)
    By L. Lerner   **49**, 49
YEATS, W. B., AND THE POETRY OF
    WAR (W)
    By T. R. Henn   **51**, 301
YORK MINSTER, A ROMANESQUE
    RELIEF IN
    By Sir E. Maclagan   **10**, 479

Date Due

			UML 735